TRUST ME I'M A CARE WORKER

TRUST ME I'M A CARE WORKER

CHRIS BULTEEL

The Book Guild Ltd

First published in Great Britain in 2019 by
The Book Guild Ltd
9 Priory Business Park
Wistow Road, Kibworth
Leicestershire, LE8 0RX
Freephone: 0800 999 2982
www.bookguild.co.uk
Email: info@bookguild.co.uk
Twitter: @bookguild

Typeset in 11pt Adobe Jenson Pro

Printed and bound in the UK by TJ International, Padstow, Cornwall

ISBN 978 1912881 710

British Library Cataloguing in Publication Data.
A catalogue record for this book is available from the British Library.

MIX
Paper from responsible sources
FSC® C013056

This book is dedicated to the 1.4 million people that work within the Social Care sector, helping those with illness or disabilities whatever the cause. They are often undervalued and poorly paid but carry out their tasks without thought for themselves, but with love for those less fortunate than themselves.

It is also dedicated to all those very many people who look after relatives and loved ones without reward, but in the knowledge that they are enhancing lives.

Above all, it is dedicated to those that need help in their daily lives. Whether physically or mentally disabled, ill or at end of life or simply lonely. They often show huge courage against adversity and often smile when they should be sad.

Contents

Introduction

Life can be full of twists and turns and my own life has been no exception. I was born to the sound of the dawn chorus on 20th April, in the year 1949. I enjoyed an idyllic childhood under the shadow of Painswick Beacon in the Cotswolds. My brother John and I would leave home on holiday mornings to go exploring, only to return when the pangs of hunger beckoned us back to the delightful home baking of Mum. We would invariably explore with such local notables as Eleanor, Judy and Ian, known collectively as the Black Hand Gang. This was a totally acceptable name in the mid 1950s but might now be considered politically incorrect. The reason for the name was the wearing of black woollen gloves that were the normal winter school uniform accessory, worn by the gang to prevent the leaving of fingerprints at the sites of the many practical jokes carried out in the community.

Membership of the gang was gained by way of an initiation rite that involved, among other acts, being able to sit on a thistle with underwear removed to assess whether any member might scream in a crisis. The rites of passage into the gang were performed in Dad's shed. The purpose of the gang never became clear, but I cannot remember it causing any distress in Upton Lane, Barnwood, Gloucester. I suppose we were just doing what was natural for six and seven-year-olds in that far distant time!

Since that time and considering reasonably poor exam results, my life has taken many twists and turns. I needed to go to college to learn a skill and managed to gain admission to Bournemouth College of Technology for a four-year sandwich course on Hotel and Catering Management, becoming a graduate of The Hotel and Catering Institute.

Before starting the course I worked on a heather farm, learning how to propagate heathers, which we then sold to local authorities in England and Scotland. I also gained knowledge on the propagation of dwarf conifers, the evidence of my success being measured by the thirty to forty foot conifers now inhabiting gardens throughout Dorset, not least in my own and my mothers gardens.

Finishing college I opted to go into the family restaurant, which prided itself on home-cooked, true English food. It was very successful, particularly the homemade fudge which we were producing at the rate of half a hundredweight per week!! Very successful, but not conducive to family life, so I sold up and became a village grocer. Many other changes took place in my life, but none more monumental than the one I'm about to describe. Back in 2002 my life took on an enormous change, one with which I initially didn't believe I could cope. Circumstances led me to leave my long-standing career in catering and enter into a new phase in my life that was to change my perspective on the world.

Although I had always been at the forefront when it came to volunteering, I never guessed that I would end up being paid to help people with all sorts of differing problems. I say paid, but I found myself receiving the minimum wage, which would only just cover my financial commitments. I very soon realised that I had become part of a vast workforce, which made a massive contribution to our society but was only just managing to survive on breadline wages.

I was grateful to have been elected as a Poole Borough councillor some years earlier, so my meagre wage was supplemented by a not too generous allowance from the council. However, that was to change over the years as I progressed through the council, becoming a committee chair and also the chair of the Dorset Fire Authority. Together with income from various government quangos, I found my public work was paying more than my day job. This enabled me to concentrate on my job as a care worker without having to worry where the next penny was coming from.

As I look back on those early years and read through my diaries, I remember all the wonderful people I helped, their life stories and their bravery in coping with various ailments and disorders that were so often life threatening. I also remember the happy times when I would laugh with them over hilarious situations or events that occurred, whilst I was administering care in as professional a manner as possible. The service users all became my friends, although sadly many have now passed away – gone to a place of endless pain-free peace.

There is an army of care support workers throughout the land, all badly paid and poorly rewarded but entirely dedicated to the people they help. They are the true unsung heroes, who rarely grumble at their lot, but instead quietly get on with the job of helping others. It is to those people that I dedicate this book, as I know they will appreciate some of my tales.

To start the process of delving through my diaries, it is necessary to go back to 2005 to one of my greatest successes – one that told me that I had finally found my niche in life. I have changed the names, locations, and in some cases the illnesses and/or disabilities, to prevent any person mentioned in this book being identified. While most have sadly passed away, there are still family members living who may not wish their loved ones to be identified.

2nd September 2005
A realisation

"Now that the wife's gone, you're more than welcome to bugger off!"

Could these really be the same words uttered less than a fortnight ago by the gentleman sitting to my left? We were enjoying the dying warmth of the hottest summer on record, consuming vanilla and nut ice cream topped with rich chocolate sauce, whilst looking out onto the tranquil waters of Poole Bay. The beach and promenade were busy with a mostly middle-aged and elderly populous, the children having returned to school from the long summer break. I wondered whether any of the people passing by, who took the time to look at us, thought for a moment about the odd couple before them, sitting in silent contemplation on identical deck chairs, savouring the delectable combination of ice cream, nuts and sticky confection.

George uttered few words and lived a life of such total inward thought and confusion that he had been diagnosed with clinical depression, anxiety and short-term memory loss.

Today however, he has lightened up and told me a little of his past life. My task, as a newly trained care worker, was to allow his wife a brief respite and get him away from his warden-assisted flat, to try to bring him out of his deep depression, which I have finally achieved today, 2nd September

2005. The surreal scene now being enacted takes my mind back to late spring three years previously when, my life having taken a dramatic turn, I saw my chosen and long-time career in the catering industry end abruptly, with dire warnings about the state of my health. Talk of life expectancy had frightened me into embarking on a totally new and unexpected career at the ripe, yet not quite old age of fifty-three. I had become a care worker.

George was to be the pivotal point in my new calling. He gave me the subliminal message that I had taken the right path in life, telling me I had begun to have a tangible success and leading me towards taking my National Vocational Qualification in Care, that would propel me forward from catering manager to fully qualified care worker. In short I had made friends with George, gained his trust and succeeded where all others had failed. I had shared an intimate moment with his muddled mind, in which I had been able to remind him that he had a past of which he could be proud.

The unexpected change in my life had become meaningful and I was about to move forward in a career that was going to make a difference to society. Within a very short space of time I had learned how to communicate with one of the most difficult of people and to make a significant improvement in his tangled life. This small victory caused me to cast my mind back to June 2004…

23rd June 2004
Jarvey brings home the bacon

This must prove to be one of my most memorable days as a care worker.

I have recently completed my initial training with a new employer, after working briefly for another organisation where I was doing nothing but personal care. I am totally unprepared for the type of assignment I have been given. Whilst before, I found myself tearing around the streets of Bournemouth from client to client, getting people up in the morning and putting them to bed at night, I now find myself part of a totally new ball game. The pressure of what I had christened the 'bum run', where each task took less than half an hour and I was given no time to travel from one address to the other, was over. This had been very stressful and hardly conducive to giving a caring impression to the client. Often I would start at seven in the morning, having finished my last appointment at 11.30pm the previous night. My next task would be at an address on the other side of town, which would be followed by one at 7.55am very close to where my first client had been. The organisers of that outfit clearly didn't possess a local street map or a timetable of the rush hour. I would often find myself in horrendous traffic jams, losing precious minutes that had to be made up by short-timing the later clients.

I was relieved to have changed my employer to one that seemed more interested in the client than the volume of business. True, the pay was a little worse, if that were possible considering the national minimum wage structure, but the stress factor had reduced to almost zero. I also felt confident that my line manager, Charlotte, was at the other end of the phone to offer help and advice. I was given clear instructions, ample travel time and concise client details. I felt that I was ready to take on anything, and the task that I had been given that day seemed to be quite straightforward, with instructions that proved to be my initiation into the home-sitting service.

'Client:-Jarvey Topper, ninety-four years young, fully mobile, needs watching at all times. On no account should you leave this client alone at any time. Jarvey suffers from the onset of senile dementia and short-term memory loss and may need help in finding the toilet. Interests include steam engines and farms. Task: sit with client for the afternoon whilst his wife goes to the hairdressers'.

I duly arrived at the appointed hour at the stated address and was immediately struck by a strong feeling of peaceful serenity surrounding the large cottage I was approaching. Red roses embraced the porch, and the vegetation clinging to the walls gave the impression that, earlier in the year, the façade of this idyllic home had been covered with bright blue wisteria. The front garden was immaculate, with neatly trimmed lawns and a gravel path totally devoid of weeds and lined with lavender bushes which gave off an exquisite aroma that pervaded the afternoon air. The thatched roof came almost to the top of the downstairs windows, of which there were four, with diamond leaded panes. These were matched by four dormer windows, which seemed to snuggle into the thatch. I approached the imposing oak door and knocked the huge lion head-shaped brass knocker. The door was opened by one of the most motherly looking characters that I have ever had the pleasure to meet: slightly plump, short of stature and possessing of a veritable thatch of snowy white hair, pulled into a bun, that topped a face that could have come straight from the pages of a Thomas Hardy novel. This was Dorset granny at her finest: a perfect face tinted with rosy cheeks and eyes sporting a tiny pair of metal-framed glasses.

"Hello, I'm Florence, and you must be Chris. Please come in and sit yourself down whilst I explain to you what has happened."

I followed her through the open door into a hall lined with carved oak panelling, which was covered from floor to ceiling with horse brasses interspersed with ancient pictures of steam engines. Bits of horse bridle and other equestrian equipment filled most available spaces, making it look more like a tack room than a cottage hallway. I was ushered into the drawing room, perfectly furnished with chintzy chairs and oak cabinets, and into a very comfortable looking rocking chair.

"Jarvey's gone walkabout," she said, so unconcerned that I presumed he must be somewhere in the back garden. "This time the silly old bugger's been gone for over two hours," she continued. "Don't know where the hell he is this time. Got the whole family looking for him at this very moment. They'll soon have to call the police, as he'll never remember where he lives, the silly old bugger."

I was completely taken aback by the language issuing from the mouth of this charming elderly lady, that seemed strangely incongruous in the surroundings of such a beautiful home.

"Does he do this often?" I asked, trying not to show my concern and surprise.

"All the bloody time," she replied. "Thinks he's still on the farm and goes off to get they cows in for a milkin'. Trouble is, we ain't got no farm nor cows anymore. Supposed to be retired we are, but not Jarvey, the silly old bugger. He still goes off two times a day to get them bloody cows in for milkin'. You'd think he'd realise that there aren't any damned cows anymore. If it isn't cows it's pigs or chickens or some other bloody job on the non-existent farm."

"What do you want me to do, then?" I asked, somewhat feebly.

"Wait till we get him back. Then lock the old bugger in the house till I get home. I'll give him the sharp end of my tongue when I see him, just you wait and see. I'm going out no matter what, but before I do I'll show you the kitchen where your tea's all laid out. Better feed him as well if he comes back, the silly old man."

With those kind words she beckoned me into a perfect cottage kitchen featuring an ancient cooking range along one wall, on which stood various pots, pans and kettles. The floor covering of red quarry tiles contrasted with walls that were painted a delicate shade of primrose. In the middle of the room stood a huge oak table, laden with delightful food, including buttered fruit scones, cakes, buttered bread, jams and clotted cream. Six wheel back chairs, and two larger carver chairs at each end, completed the rustic scene. The aroma that excited the taste buds gave evidence that all before me had been baked earlier, on the range.

"Help yourself when you're ready," she ordered, "and feed the silly old bugger when he comes back."

With that she said goodbye and left me alone in this strange environment. Hearing the front door slam as she left for her appointment, I was left stunned and silent, pondering what to do next. It was clear that I must stay where I was in case Jarvey returned. I had been given the keys to lock him in when he came home, and I also had the phone number of his daughter, which I rang immediately. No answer. She must have been out looking for Jarvey. To say that I was bemused by the situation would be a gross understatement, standing as I was in a strange kitchen in an idyllic country cottage, surrounded by home-baked delicacies and looking after some man who wasn't there. Perhaps I should phone the office.

"Who be you and what be ee doin' 'ere?"

I was startled by the suddenness of the words and the deep Dorset dialect (that I find almost impossible to put into the written word). I turned to find myself confronted by an extraordinary man, whose stoop belied a height that must have exceeded six feet had he been standing upright. He wore a pair of dark brown cord trousers and a tweed jacket that seemed to have leather patches on every available pressure point, beneath which was a worn chequered shirt. Upon his head was a very worn flat cap, topping a face that bore the resemblance of a weathered prune, the wrinkles of which gave him such a scowl that I felt sure it could never be broken by a smile. He gave the impression that he had spent his entire life in the fields, so intimately close to nature that he could almost merge into the countryside.

"You must be Jarvey," I replied, wondering where the search party was and how he had managed to get back home seemingly unaided.

"Course I am, you silly ol' bugger," he said, as if I should have known instantly who he was. "But who the hell are you and what be ee doin' in my kitchen? And where in the bloody hell is Florrie?"

I sensed that this was not going to be the easiest of afternoons so, by way of conversation, I asked meekly, "Where have you been?"

"You must be as daft as a brush! What a crazy question," came the abrupt reply. "I've bin gettin' in they thar cows for a milkin'. Bin getting' in the hay an' all. Now all that's left is the pigs an' hens. Then we'll all be able to 'ave our tea and go to bed."

He left the kitchen and made for the drawing room, where he promptly sat down and took off his hat. Then he stood up and put his hat back on – then sat down again and removed the hat once more. This ritual was repeated many times, until he finally seemed to settle, during which time I had taken the precaution of locking all the doors. Having got him inside the cottage I wasn't going to let him go… or so I thought. That was the plan and, as we all know, the best-laid plans can go badly wrong. However, I sat with him and explained who I was, why I was there and where Florence had gone, explaining that she would be back shortly and then all would be back to normal. He seemed to take everything in, and I was feeling rather proud that I had managed to make this unusual character understand me. Perhaps I was going to do quite well in this job, having suddenly found that I could access the mind of someone with the onset of dementia. He fully understood who I was, where I was from and had no doubt that I was a care worker looking after his interests whilst his long-suffering wife gained some essential respite.

"Who be you and why be ee 'ere?" I was shattered to hear.

I then went through the whole process again.

"But where be Florrie? And who be you?" Maybe I had been too sure of my abilities.

This was repeated many times until I eventually came to the conclusion that he was never going to know who I was or why I was there. It did, however, teach me that patience was one of the attributes needed to be a successful care worker.

I guided him into the kitchen, feeling that afternoon tea would give some relief from the endless questions, and as I sat him down at the large kitchen table he began to repeat the ritual of standing and sitting whilst removing and replacing his hat. I became increasingly aware that he wasn't comfortable in my presence and that he was looking for a means to escape, moving from room to room, calling out his wife's name, while I followed him around the cottage in an almost manic pursuit of someone who wasn't there. He asked for the toilet and I showed him upstairs. He asked for the other toilet and pointed to the back garden. I showed him the outside toilet and left him to do his best whilst I returned to the kitchen to make a pot of tea. I should have been alerted by his last words: "Gotta get they pigs in," as he locked himself in the outside loo.

It quickly dawned on me that Jarvey had somehow managed to escape once more and I had failed in my duty. I searched the immediate area, but Jarvey was gone, vanished into thin air. What should I do next, apart from panic? No one knew that he had returned. I could pretend that I had spent the whole afternoon waiting for him and that he had failed to materialise. With that thought on my mind I sat down guiltily at the kitchen table and, in a robotic, confused state, helped myself to the baked delicacies that surrounded me. Time passed in a blur as I became increasingly concerned for his safety. I paced about nervously, wondering what to do next. I phoned the daughter again, but there was still no reply. I imagined the whole village looking for this man, looking for his wife, looking for pigs and cows that didn't really exist. In the midst of all this chaos was a care worker who had failed in his duty. This was going to be the end of a very short career.

With these thoughts in my mind I had lost track of time and decided that I must call the office to tell them all that had happened. As I picked up the phone I vaguely heard the sound of an approaching car and looked out of the window to see Florence rounding the corner of the cottage. I went outside and, to my astonishment, found Jarvey, beckoning his wife towards the open doors of the garage. As he held the door open with his left hand, his right arm waved the car into its resting place, whereupon he closed and locked the garage doors, Florence still in the car, with the unforgettable words:

"There, that's got they ruddy pigs in! That's brought home the bacon!"

I decided to get him back in the cottage first, and then released Florence from her imprisonment. A huge feeling of relief came over me and I realised that there were lessons to be learnt. I never went back to the home of the Toppers and can only assume that he either died or went into a care home. However, I shall never forget Jarvey and my initiation into the home-sitting service.

24th August 2004
Where's the cheese?

Dealing with dementia can be very hard at times, but the most difficult person I have ever had to deal with was Nigel Crawley. He lived alone in a bungalow in the suburbs of Poole, and was still at home simply because his daughter was trying to protect her inheritance. Going into a dementia care home would cost over £1,000 a week, and his meagre savings would soon be gone and his home sold to pay the heavy bills. I was the cheap option, my care organisation charging well under £100 for my daily visit.

My tasks were to ensure that he was okay, that he had fed himself and washed properly. I also had to remind him which day of the week it was, to take his medication or do his shopping. The shopping was the most difficult task, as whenever I asked him what he needed he would reply, "A new car would be nice, and perhaps a modern lawnmower." Needless to say, I only bought the essential household goods and a balanced diet of food. I often wondered why his daughter didn't help with these things, as she lived only a couple of miles away. When I did occasionally see her she would have a list of complaints about the care received.

One of Nigel's biggest problems was that after I had put everything away from the shopping trips, he would relocate them and rearrange them around the bungalow. This included foodstuffs that should be kept in the fridge. It was my task every morning to look in every drawer and every cupboard to locate his food and return it to its proper place. One morning, I arrived at the allotted time and asked him if he had eaten any breakfast.

"No," came the reply. "I couldn't find anything. If you're going shopping I would love a toasted cheese."

Knowing that the day before I had bought both bread and cheese I had to locate their whereabouts. I found a loaf of bread in his sock drawer but failed to locate the cheese.

"Have you any idea where the cheese has gone?" I asked, with little hope of getting a sensible answer.

"It's in the usual place," came the unexpected answer. "It's in the garden where all cheese should be kept."

I searched the garden and eventually found a new and still wrapped piece of the finest cheddar cheese. It looked unharmed, despite the fact that it had spent the last twenty-four hours in the garden shed. I checked it closely to satisfy myself that rodents hadn't even sniffed it, and then proceeded to make him his cheese on toast. I stayed with him until he had finished his rather peculiar breakfast as, if I had left him, the food would probably have ended up in the wardrobe.

I knew that Nigel was very concerned about the state of his garden, which at one time must have been an absolute picture, but nothing prepared me for the sight that greeted me on another morning call. Having decided that the hedges were getting a little overgrown he had given them a trim. However, the use of an upright Hoover vacuum cleaner was not the obvious choice of cutting implement. He was holding the cleaner aloft and trying to trim the hedge by vacuum power. When I tried to stop him he insisted that what he was doing was sensible and would get the task done, as it would suck up the offending branches. I had to turn off the power in an attempt to stop him injuring himself and phoned the office to ask whether they could arrange some garden help.

They did try, but eventually his daughter sent her sons along to do the job, in order to save money – and ultimately her inheritance.

Poor Nigel passed away eighteen months later. He never went into full-time care and a 'for sale' notice appeared outside his house within a week of his death. His last years were not happy and I wondered how a family could act in such a callous way to someone who had loved them and given his life to them. The onset of dementia was not his fault; and at a time when he needed support and love, he was denied both. I only hope that my brief time with him helped him in some small way.

19th August 2005

Try, try and try again!

Visiting a new client for the first time can be a stressful event, whereby the care worker can never be sure how he will welcomed, or indeed *if* he will welcomed. The client details give scant information and give no indication of a person's character or interests in life. We go to meet a complete stranger, often with mental problems, with our eyes closed, and have to learn as we go along. Today has been such a day.

I have been instructed to visit George to give him some meaningful company whilst his wife has a little respite. The client details warn me of a nervous dog and alert me to the fact that George can be a little abrupt and suffers from depression, short-term memory loss and anxiety, which is nothing unusual in my line of work. Should the visit be a success, I am to visit on a regular basis and try to bring him out of his depressive shell.

The ferocious barking that greeted my light knock on the door should have warned me that this was not going to be the most welcoming of households. His wife, June, answered the door and let loose the hound from hell, which turned out to be a tiny terrier that could jump nearly as high as my knees. He did, however, possess a vicious little nip with his needle-sharp fangs. The onslaught on my ankles continued for a full five minutes, whilst his mistress shouted at me, trying to be heard above the canine cacophony.

"Don't worry!" she shouted. "His bark's worse than his bite!" You could have fooled me.

"He'll soon settle down," she continued. "He just has to get used to you."

I was instructed to sit, which I did, and the biting turned into a frenzied attempt to copulate with my lower left leg. This was clearly going to be a visit with a difference. Once June had seen the sense of shutting the ferocious and sex-starved beast away in the kitchen we were able to engage in some civilised talk, if such a one-sided conversation could be classified as civilised. I quickly realised why George said so little; he simply wasn't given the opportunity to reply. I began to sympathise with him and realised that one of the main causes of his anxiety was his wife.

"I'm going out to town," she started. "I hope that all will be well, assuming you're trained to deal with difficult old buggers like my George."

"I'm well used to—" I started to say, as she interrupted with, "Cos he's bloody awkward and almost impossible to talk to; got this feeling that everyone's against him, lazy old sod that he is to be sure. He never does much communicating nor talking, just sits in that bloody chair from morning till night doing nothing but feel damned sorry for himself; coffee is in the kitchen and biscuits are in the tin, not that he'll want anything, won't even ask if he does, only frets that no one ever does anything for him. I'll be gone for two hours or more and if I'm not back in time just leave the old codger on his own… Oh! And if you take him out, please try to lose him, *permanently*!"

With that said, she got up and left the flat, leaving me temporarily stunned that anyone could talk for so long without pausing for breath.

"Now that the wife's gone you're more than welcome to bugger off," said George as soon as the sound of her retreating footsteps faded.

This was not going to be the easiest of days!

"Your wife has a very strong character," I ventured to suggest in as diplomatic a way as possible.

"Don't want to talk about her. Likes the sound of her own voice far too much. This is the one time I get for a bit of peace and quiet, and you show up. Well, you can either sit there and shut up, or you can bugger off."

I realised that my visit was not purely for company, but to make sure that he was okay and free from danger. People with short-term memory loss can be very dangerous to themselves if left alone, making such mundane tasks as lighting a cigarette or putting something on the cooker a very hazardous exercise.

I well remember the time I was sitting with a client in his kitchen. He had decided that he would make the coffee and all went well until he reached into the cupboard under the sink, only to extract a bottle of fabric conditioner, which he had thought was the milk. People often forget what they have just done, with potentially disastrous results. They could also decide to go for a walk and forget where they are or where they live. I had to suffer the full two hours with someone who didn't want me there and had absolutely no intention of carrying out any form of sensible communication.

I tried to make polite conversation, asking him such mundane questions as: did he have any interests, hobbies, favourite television programmes, card games, board games, etc.? His answer was clear in the extreme.

"I'll tell you here and now that I have absolutely no interests and have never played card games or anything silly like that. I have no desire to go anywhere, read anything or watch pointless television programmes. I don't like any sort of music, never read and have no intention of saying anything about my past. In short, I am probably the most boring person you are ever likely to meet and if you insist on sitting here with me I would ask that you do so in total silence."

That being said, I felt I had no option but to agree with him and say no more. I sat with him for the allotted two hours, made my excuses and left, with the jovial parting, "See you on Friday."

"Not if I can bloody help it," he shouted as I closed the door.

Mental problems can affect people in very different ways, and this client was obviously going to be a problem. My only hope in the short term was that his memory was so bad that by Friday he would have forgotten who I was. Memory loss can be a real impediment to the sufferer, but a huge benefit to the carer. In the case of George I was simply going to have to try, try and try again until I could gain his respect and friendship. If things didn't work out I would place it in my diary as another case of utter failure. Whilst I did have huge successes with some clients, I also experienced times when, whatever I did, I failed to get through to them. However, I had taken a great liking to George for being so honest in his feelings about carers, and me in general. I was determined to break through his barriers and reach a situation where he looked forward to my visits.

Whilst driving back to the office, I thought back to the various cases of memory loss I had had to deal with over my short time as a care worker. My thoughts turned to July of last year, when I had been looking after my old chums, Bill and Ben. Both were now in permanent care, but whilst I had been looking after them they had become firm friends.

3rd July 2004
Bill and Ben

Today I have visited Bill and Ben, both of whom suffer from varying degrees of dementia, a strange ailment that defies all logical explanation. During my work I come into contact with many sufferers and notice that in almost every case they have led rich and fruitful lives, following occupations that required great mental dexterity and intelligence. It is almost as if they have worn out a vital part of their brain in the same way that an athlete can wear out parts of their body.

The first emotion I always felt in dealing with these cases was one of acute sadness, then concern for myself that I would be unable to communicate with them. I took the totally unreasoned approach that they were, in some way, mentally unstable and therefore virtually impossible to work with in any meaningful way.

As care workers, we have little preparation for what to expect of such people. Our training is initially brief as it in no way covers the intricacies of psychology and the workings of the human brain. Were we able to be so trained, I guess we would all be doctors or brain surgeons and not just humble care workers. The best training that we ever undertake is hands-on experience. However, despite this lack of expertise and knowledge, I soon found myself intrigued by this crippling ailment and surprised that I was able to cope quite easily, probably helped by the fact that I only had to spend a couple of hours a week with my newfound friends. I have huge admiration for the partners of these lost souls, who have to live with the disability for twenty-four hours of every single day, and long for just two hours of respite a week. I always made it my task, wherever possible, to take the client away from the home environment to give the full-time carer a proper, albeit brief, degree of relief.

I had expected to be received with some degree of suspicion but soon found that if you displayed warmth and understanding to them, they would repay you in the same way. It took me by surprise that they would soon get to know me personally and be waiting for me when I arrived on my weekly visit. I found that they possessed an almost childlike quality, an innocent charm that belied their years and undoubted experience of life. Bill and Ben were just such people. I would engage them in conversation that lasted for the full two hours of my visits, and whilst I became aware of their respective backgrounds I was far more interested in the stories of their early years.

They had both been very successful in life. Bill had been involved with electrical manufacturing in a very big way and now lived, with his wife Sue, in a penthouse apartment overlooking Poole Bay, with stunning views of the Purbeck Hills and the Isle of Wight. He little appreciated this and rarely looked out of the windows. On returning after our walk or drive, he would invariably ask why we were going into such an impressive block of flats. He failed to remember where he lived, and it sometimes took him a while to realise that the lady answering the door was his wife. Within two hours he had forgotten where he lived and yet had spoken enthusiastically about his early passion for classic motorbikes, remembering them all and talking with pinpoint accuracy of the workings and capabilities of such machines as Nortons, Triumphs, Ariels and BSAs. He had owned them all in his youth and had great knowledge of them.

Ben was equally successful and lived with his wife, Hazel, in a large, newly built bungalow on the edge of the Dorset countryside. He was what is known as a 'runner' and would sometimes escape his home environment to go for an innocent walk, forget where he was, or indeed who he was, and just carry on walking. This would often lead to a search party involving friends, neighbours, relatives and the police. I had to be very careful not to let him out of my sight. Ben had been at the top of the educational profession, but spoke little of this, his passions having been scouting and cycling, and he would spend hours telling me of his mammoth cycle trips and his happy years in and leading the scouts.

These gentle souls, steeped in childlike innocence, could be immensely rewarding mentally. They had lost their self-consciousness and so opened up to me with a pure trust that I found endearing. This was no longer just a job; it was providing me with a large measure of mental enrichment. I had often felt that it was a shame that children ever had to grow up, and now I was finding a group of people who had found mental solace from their stressful lives by returning to their childhood. They no longer needed to keep up appearances, no longer had to cope with the stress and the hurly-burly of modern life. Neither had a mobile phone, and the technology of the day had passed them by. They simply didn't need all that. I began to envy them in some small way, though I never forgot the stress that this put on their partners, and rather selfishly thought that I would not mind if I found myself suffering from such a disability – but secretly prayed that my wife would never be so afflicted.

Just like children, Bill and Ben could provide me with much pleasure but could also cause acute embarrassment. Both, at some time or other, did something that not only embarrassed me but also put me in acute danger of being accused of some act of gross indecency, which usually involved their natural functions. As far as the simple process of going to the toilet was concerned, they were quite capable of remembering what to do when the urge to perform took hold. However, just like children, they had to be reminded to 'use the loo' before leaving home. This they always did to order, but again, just like children, they would sometimes get caught short just down the road, which would necessitate a speedy return to base.

One day I had taken Bill to the beach for a walk along the promenade and as soon as we arrived he expressed a need for a wee. We made a dash for the public toilet, and I stood beside him at the urinal. It soon became clear that the dementia had set in and he had completely forgotten how to extricate himself from his trousers, which conjured up vivid images of very wet trousers and equally wet car seats. This meant that, with no change of clothing available, I was going to have to act quickly.

As a care worker I am well used to dealing with gentlemen who have such disabilities that they need help to perform their bodily functions. I have been trained for such eventualities and deal with them swiftly, clinically and with some measure of expertise. I always carried a pair of surgical gloves in my pocket, as it would be unwise, both professionally and health-wise, to touch any private part of the anatomy with bare hands. I quickly assessed the situation as I was automatically pulling on my latex gloves and, noting that the toilet was empty apart from us, I realised I was going to have to assist Bill before nature took its inevitable course, so I deftly unzipped his trousers and reached inside.

To my utter horror I found that he had put his Y-fronts on back to front and the hole for the extraction of his member was inaccessible. I needed to look closer at the problem so turned him to face me so that I could kneel and try to relieve the situation, but as I reached inside his trousers I sensed that we were not alone. I glanced up and became aware that I was being closely scrutinised by a uniformed beach warden. For a while I knelt there in silence, my face reddening to a deep scarlet, as if caught in some obscene act. The warden glared at me with his mouth wide open, seemingly unable to take in the enormity of the situation he was witnessing. As he reached for his radio I realised that I had to act quickly to avoid the possibility of imminent arrest, and uttered the unforgettable words, "Trust me, I'm a care worker!" Luckily I was carrying my ID badge and was able, after some considerable explanation, to get myself out of a very tricky situation.

And Bill? He seemed totally and blissfully bemused by the whole situation and just smiled at me with an incredibly innocent grin. He had obviously forgotten the need for a wee. We set off, chuckling to ourselves as we walked along our happy way. I determined that, in the future, I would always take a client to an enclosed cubicle, lock the door and ignore the looks of the men who heard me talking to another male within the locked cubicle of a public loo. It has certainly changed my perspective of public toilets, and I now realise that there is sometimes a logical explanation for the strange behaviour of some of their patrons!

This experience not only made my outings safer, but also made me aware that any amount of training can never prepare you for the unexpected. Only experience will do that, and never again would I find myself in such an embarrassing and potentially damaging situation... or so I thought! I had bargained without the eccentricities of Ben.

One day I had decided to take him for a walk in the local forest, an area he loved and where we had been many times before without any problems. As usual, I had ensured that he had used the toilet before leaving home, but on arrival at our destination he complained that he needed to go again, which meant that I had to find a safe place for him to perform his bodily functions away from the public gaze.

There appeared to be no one around, so I guided him to a dense thicket and told him I would keep watch, but as soon as he disappeared I was concerned to see, rounding the corner of the path, a pair of large horses on which were mounted a pair of equally large and fearsome-looking ladies. I called out to Ben to be careful as people were approaching. True to form he obeyed my call and finished what he was doing before returning to my side. As the horses drew near, I was aware of a look of abject horror and disgust on the faces of the two ladies.

"Disgraceful behaviour; you ought to be arrested!" said one in a stern voice as they passed.

What had I done to cause such outrage? Did I look guilty of some seedy perversion? Had Ben's emergence from the bushes given the impression that something really evil had been going on between us?

We walked in silence, pondering on the offence so obviously caused to the two angry ladies, when I became aware of the reason for their distress. As I glanced down I noticed that Ben had failed to 'put Percy back in his pants' and that his manhood was swinging with free abandon in the fresh spring air. I quickly addressed the situation and beat a hasty retreat to the safety of the car before the police sirens began to wail.

16th July 2004

How extraordinary!

It is very odd that, in times gone by, people became known by names that were at total variance with their christened moniker. My client details always gave the Christian name of the person concerned, whilst my training warned me never to use the familiarity of a first name until I had gained consent to do so. I was always wary of how to address a client until I had covered certain ground rules, and I learned very quickly never to take things at face value. The Mr Wards nearly always seemed to be called Sharkey, Mr Whites answered to Chalky, Mr Millers to Dusty and Mr Clarkes were nearly always referred to as Nobby, regardless of their first names. I also mused on the change in pronunciation of the first names; for example, Sean was pronounced as Shaun, and Shellagh as Sheila, all of which made my life, as a care worker, more complicated than was perhaps necessary. There were many other examples that I came across during my employment, but none so notable as Mr Ralph Pembleton-Smythe.

One day in mid-July I was called to a flat, overlooking the sea, in an exclusive road in Southbourne. As I drove through the impressive wrought-iron gates I became aware of a tall lady with the most beautifully styled silver hair, beckoning me to park in a particular bay. This rather surprised me as there were at least twelve bays, none of which seemed to be marked, and there was not another car in sight. I duly parked and wound down the window.

"I say, old chap, you must be Chris. I checked with your office to ask the colour of your car just to make sure I was looking out for the right person. They told me gold, and I suppose it could be described as a rather brash gold, though I would rather call it a rather common yellow. Would you mind awfully turning it round to face the other way? We have to look out on this car park from our kitchen windows and it is so much more pleasant to see the cars' faces rather than their bottoms, don't you think?"

This was Hyacinth Bucket at her finest. The clipped and very false tone of her voice, the immaculately manicured hands, coupled with the slightly upturned nose gave the distinct impression of an aspiring Lady of the Manor.

"You must be Mrs Pembleton-Smythe," I asked, feeling rather foolish for stating the obvious.

"I am indeed the lady of the house. But we don't need to stand on ceremony in this house, so please call me Iris."

I just knew that she had to be named after a flower!

"After all, you may be a care worker, but that doesn't make you a servant. I understand from your office that you are also a councillor. I did particularly ask for a better class of care worker and I think you would agree that it is far better, should the need arise of course, to introduce you to one's friends as a councillor rather than just a plain care worker."

I was astounded by the snobbery of this lady and stated that I would much rather be introduced as just plain Chris, a care worker who is proud to be doing the job that he has.

"So be it, Councillor," she replied, totally ignoring what I had just said. "Now, please come in and meet my husband, and don't stand on ceremony. He likes his friends to call him by his Christian name."

As we made our way up the stairs she gave me the clearest of instructions. I was to sit with Mr Pembleton-Smythe for three hours whilst she went to the local Ladies' Circle to play a game of bridge. Mr Pembleton-Smythe suffered from acute short-term memory loss and occasionally wondered who he was. Conversation might be a little one-sided and he would tend to repeat himself, forgetting what he had said in the previous sentence.

"One thing he never forgets is that 'the sun goes over the yardarm' at 11am precisely. He will instinctively ask for some sort of alcoholic beverage."

On no account was I to bow to his demands and let him near the gin bottle. Coffee and shortbread were served at 10.30am precisely and sandwiches were prepared and in the refrigerator with iced lemonade. On no account was I to accept that they always enjoyed a glass of claret at this time; it was simply untrue and yet another ruse to get at the alcohol.

"If you find yourself getting bored, please feel free to get out the bagatelle as Mr Pembleton-Smythe loves a game. Don't be fooled into giving him a glass of beer at this stage, despite his protestations that he always enjoys beer whilst playing bagatelle, just like he did at the local hostelry. On no account let him near the alcohol."

We entered the lounge to be met by the striking figure of Mr Pembleton-Smythe.

"Good morning, Ralph," I said cheerfully. "I'm Chris from the care organisation."

"Oh dear no!" exclaimed Iris. "The name is Raif, not Ralph!"

I wondered once more on the peculiarity of not pronouncing the name as it was spelt but putting a totally different slant on it, as if it made Ralph a little less common.

"And I told Raif that you were from the council, not from the care organisation. He doesn't like care workers."

Raif was a splendid figure of an upper-class twit sort of man, meant in the kindest possible way. He appeared to be a man who had never done a proper day's work in his life and who had forgotten to take a toffee out of his mouth whilst speaking. He peered at me over his metal-framed half-moon glasses, as if examining something rather unpleasant.

"How extraordinary," he said. "I was expecting someone from the care organisation and you turn up completely out of the blue. Where are you from? I don't recall having met you before. Are you from the council?"

"No, Raif, I'm a care worker." I quickly realised my mistake and corrected myself, "No! I mean, I'm from the council!"

"How extraordinary," he said. "I was expecting someone from the care organisation and you turn up completely out of the blue. Where are you from? I don't recall having met you before. Are you from the council?"

"No Raif, I'm a care worker." I quickly realised my mistake again and corrected myself, "No… I mean I'm from the council."

"How extraordinary. I was expecting someone from the council and then they send a bloody care worker. Can't stand care workers as I don't need them, don't you know. Still extraordinary though, expecting someone from the care council and now you turn up and surprise me. Tell me, who are you again?"

"I'm Chris, a care worker from the council!" I said, covered in confusion.

"Good gracious, how extraordinary. I was expecting someone from the council and you turn up. The name's Chris, is it?" Progress at last. "Why are you here, then? I was really expecting someone from the council. But whilst you are here, and considering that the sun has gone over the yardarm, do you fancy a drink? I always enjoy a glass or three around this time of the morning. Perhaps a stiff G&T would go down rather well. Easy on the T, plenty of ice and lemon and lots of the G, don't you know. How about it, Clive? I suppose you RAF chaps are allowed to drink on duty, aren't you?

"Never mind, I always say that rules are there to be broken. Don't you agree, Wing Commander? This really is strange, Nobby; I was just thinking that I was expecting someone from the council and you turn up after all these years. Do you remember those sorties we used to go on all those years ago against the Jerries? How very extraordinary. Now, how about that bloody gin?"

"No, thank you," I said, still thoroughly confused and beginning to wonder who I really was. "I'm Chris from the council and I've come to keep you company for a while."

"How extraordinary. I was expecting my old friend Nobby to call and here you are from the council. How would you fancy a nice cool beer? There's plenty in the fridge."

I became aware that I was now alone with this strange man, Iris having left so quietly that I hadn't noticed her absence.

"My wife tells everyone that I don't touch alcohol, don't you know. Bloody liar she is. I love the stuff and can't get enough of it. Now, how about that scotch. Easy on the water and heavy on the scotch is what I always say."

As he continued to rattle on in a highly confused way, I took note of my new surroundings. The entire lounge looked as if it had been furnished in the late fifties or early sixties. The three-piece suite was covered in heavy two-tone green brocade that was so uncomfortable and hard that I felt sure it would leave permanent indentations on my bottom. A teak dresser spanning one wall sported highly polished silver and family photographs. The only other furniture were a cabinet, which I assumed housed a television set, a large radiogram, two Dralon-covered chairs, a nest of three tables and a leather-covered drinks table by each chair. The ornaments on the mantelpiece were expensive and select, and a large ebony clock supported by two huge elephants stood in the centre. The room was immaculate and I guessed that the lack of books indicated that there was a study in another part of the flat.

"How extraordinary." – I was jolted out of my daydreaming – "How one can be expecting someone to arrive and then someone totally different appears? You never know what's going to happen next. That's what makes life so interesting, don't you think? Never know what's around the next corner, so to speak, if you know what I mean. There I was expecting an old RAF chum to turn up and here you are from the bank, and my dear wife was expecting someone from the council. Fancy a drink, old chap?"

"No thanks, I'm fine; and I'm Chris from the council," I replied.

"You won't like it here, you know. Can't get a f*****g drink nowadays. Not at all like it used to be, don't you know. Bloody people banned the alcohol years ago. Makes a poor fellow pretty desperate, don't you know."

I felt that I had to change the subject.

"Did you used to be in the RAF?"

Pretty stupid question with a pretty obvious answer, I thought to myself as I surveyed the wartime photos of Ralph in his RAF uniform adorning the walls.

"Too bloody right, old boy. Damned good time fighting the Hun. Which squadron was yours? I was with 622 Bomber Command, but flew everything. Now, how about that drink."

"Good gracious," I replied, "it's half past ten already and time for coffee."

I left to search for the kitchen. My first hunch proved right as I opened the wrong door to reveal a study crammed from floor to ceiling with leather-bound books that would have been equally at home in the library of some stately home.

When I eventually found the kitchen I was surprised to find it rather spartan. The only concession to the 20th century were fitted 'Daisy maid' units around the kitchen sink that reminded me of the first attempts at fitted kitchens in the early sixties. There was a lack of the usual gadgets such as an electric kettle, and I soon realised that I would have to use the old method of placing a kettle on the cooker to boil the water. I half expected to find a coffee percolator but was pleasantly surprised to spy a jar of Maxwell House instant coffee in the cupboard. I peeked inside the tea caddy and was not in the least surprised to find tealeaves rather than bags. Coffee duly made, I proceeded back to the lounge.

"How nice to meet you, young man. I was just saying to the chap from the council before you came in that I was expecting someone from the bank, and in you walk. How thoughtful of you to bring coffee with you. Don't suppose you thought of brandy as well, old chap? Never mind, the wife keeps it locked in that cabinet. Be a good fellow and find the key, would you?"

I made pretence of looking for a key, but thankfully to no avail.

"Sorry, Raif, can't find it. We'll have to wait until the wife arrives. In the meantime let's enjoy our coffee, shall we?"

He, very reluctantly, accepted my invitation and we sat for the next half an hour trying to decide who I was and from whence I came. In the end I gave up as he concluded:

"Life can be very odd sometimes. I was told that you were a councillor who worked as a care worker, and here you are, a bloody abstemious vicar. Never mind, old fellow. I can take a hint. No bloody drink this morning, what? Maybe we could play a short game of bagatelle, though? Suppose you vicars don't play for cash, boring old sods that you all are. Well, if you won't have a little flutter, how about a nice cool beer?"

We then played bagatelle for the next hour, and I was relieved that I hadn't agreed to a little gamble as he won every game, cheating unmercifully by tilting the board every time he shot his ball so that it always ended up in the highest-scoring slots. Every time he did this he made the excuse that the bagatelle board was not quite level. Funny how it always seemed level when it was my go. However, letting him win seemed to take his mind off the alcohol. We became so engrossed in our game that I completely forgot the time, and we only just managed to bolt down our sandwiches and lemonade before Iris returned.

"Hello boys, how have you been?"

"Bloody well, thank you," replied Raif. "This Charlie chap is very good company, don't you know. Bloody useless at bagatelle, and very unusual to find a vicar who is so obsessed with alcohol. Been trying to find the key to the drinks cabinet all morning. I told him you had it in your bag, but he insisted that there must be a spare somewhere. Made him drink coffee and lemonade instead, poor chap. But now you're home perhaps you can give him the key."

I made my excuses and left for my next assignment.

7th April 2007
I'm so superior to you!

Remembering the sheer snobbery of the Pembleton-Smythes, I was once again subjected to the most blatant case of superiority complex when I took Jonathan for a walk along Poole seafront. Jonathan, or Jon as he liked to be addressed, had recently retired from a very important career in the City, where he was a leading light at the top of a well-known bank. He had retired early to some considerable opulence following an accident that seriously impaired his mobility.

Jon and his wife Debra were a charming couple who treated everyone in the same way, no matter what their social status. They lived in one of the most exclusive parts of Canford Cliffs in Poole, home to many millionaires. Their flat was the last word in luxury. The kitchen was so large it could have doubled as a ballroom. Every one of the four bedrooms had an en-suite bathroom, and there was another bathroom available just in case. Debra, whenever I arrived, was always in the kitchen making some sort of preserve, and often gave me a jar of her homemade marmalade, which was absolutely divine. I got on very well with them and went to see them every week to take Jon out for a car ride or a walk. He needed someone with him at all times to try to prevent a fall.

After some years with the care organisation, I became aware that, when some of the referrals within the wealthier parts of Poole were carried out, I was welcomed warmly. This was because of my supposed status within the community as a local councillor. It was felt that, as I often appeared in the local press, people might already know me. I didn't mind this but felt that it was somehow wrong to use my public life as a plus whilst I was still employed as a care worker – the same as my care worker colleagues. However, I was soon to find that my supposed status made no difference whatsoever in certain circumstances.

Today I had taken Jon for a walk along the promenade. He was in very good form and we decided to walk all the way to Bournemouth Pier, where we would enjoy a coffee and some cake before our return. He walked at a reasonably fast pace, as though he was trying to catch himself up. I had serious difficulty in keeping up with him and had to keep reminding him of his disability and warn of the possibility of a fall. However, we reached the pier and enjoyed our coffee and chocolate gateau.

Thankfully, the return trip was somewhat slower, and it seemed that Jon knew everyone along the way, nodding and giving them a hearty 'good morning' as they passed. A couple approached who were clearly very friendly with Jon and they stopped for a chat. I was introduced to them, and when he said, "This is Chris," they duly shook my hand in greeting. However, when he then said, "He is my official carer," they literally turned their backs on me and left without another word.

I assume that some people think that anyone working in the care sector is somehow inferior to everyone else, or that they have some communicable disease. They fail to appreciate that some day they may need care themselves and will inevitably get a person who is poorly paid and at the lower end of the social spectrum, but who will provide the best care to anyone, no matter what their class or social standing.

Some years ago, whilst I was still in the catering trade, it was my honour to prepare tea for a well-known duke. He had come to Poole to visit the RNLI, and I was to provide tea at the local masonic hall.

After the necessary checks by the security services, and much activity from the most wonderful sniffer dogs, all was ready to receive the duke.

As usual I had donned my best suit, as I felt the occasion demanded some formality. My staff were all dressed in black and white, and all was ready. The duke entered the room and approached me, as he obviously thought I was the organiser of the event.

"Good afternoon, and how do you do?" he said in a very pleasant tone. "And what lodge do you belong to?" he continued.

"Oh, I don't belong to any lodge here," I said. "I am the caterer."

"Oh, how nice," he replied and promptly turned his back on me.

Oh well, I didn't really have the time for a chat anyway!

29th July 2004

A lunch date to remember!

Today is a very special day in my life and one to be remembered for various reasons.

I had spoken to my boss Sandra a week previously, explaining that I needed to take at least four hours off the following week as I had a luncheon appointment that I really couldn't get out of.

"What are you doing this time? Something to do with the council, no doubt."

"Actually, I have been invited to lunch at the Lighthouse Theatre and will hopefully be enjoying such delicacies as mini pork and leek sausages, devils on horseback, asparagus and Serrano ham parcels on mini toasts, smoked salmon and ginger nigiri with soy sauce, together with lots of other delicacies and loads of wine. Oh! And I will be meeting the Queen!"

"I've heard some excuses in my time but never anything that comes close to this. Lunch with the Queen? How come?"

I then showed her the invitation, which was very posh and bore the crest of the Borough of Poole. It stated that I was invited to attend a reception at the Lighthouse, Poole, in the gracious presence of Her Majesty the Queen and His Royal Highness the Duke of Edinburgh. The invitation had come from The Worshipful the Mayor of the Borough and County of the Town of Poole.

Her Majesty was conducting the re-opening of the theatre after an extensive refit. She had originally opened the theatre some years back. I also had to admit that the invitation came as the result of a ballot amongst councillors, which gave two members the opportunity to attend. I had been a lucky winner, together with my great friend Judy Butt.

However, today my mind is on other things. I have just visited Cecil, to get him out of bed, administer a shower and get him dried and dressed and fed before I can rush back home to throw on a suit and tie. Poor old Cecil, who had unfortunately had both his legs amputated, had experienced what can only be described as an unfortunate accident during the night. He was very tearful and apologetic, but I assured him that his lack of lower limbs had made it impossible for him to reach the toilet. I also added that everyone had to use the toilet and that it was nothing unusual.

As I was cleaning up him and the bed, I couldn't help but wonder what Her Majesty would think if she knew where the hand she was likely to shake had been only a short time before. I had never been so furious with a scrubbing brush before, as I remembered my first meeting with the Queen many years previously, when I had caused quite a stir. I wondered whether she would recognise me, but as I was only six years old the previous time I doubted that I looked the same, and she must have met millions of people in the years between meetings.

In 1953 the entire neighbourhood had descended on the household of the editor of the *Gloucester Citizen*, Mr Robertson. He was the only resident in Upton Lane who possessed the luxury of a television, and we were all there to watch the coronation of Queen Elizabeth II on the tiny black and white screen that was the focal point of his lounge. I well remember that, at four years old, I wasn't that interested and, together with my young friends, caused much annoyance to the adults trying to concentrate on the lavish event. I didn't see much of the ceremony but do remember seeing the Queen at the end, holding a sceptre and golden orb, wearing a fur-lined cloak and sporting a very expensive-looking crown. This is just the image that any four-year-old would expect of a queen or princess as depicted in fairy tales.

Two years later, on 3rd May 1955 to be precise, I was enjoying the start of my third term at The King's School, Gloucester, and was now just six years old and among the youngest pupils at the school. It also coincided with the 800th anniversary of the granting of the charter to Gloucester by King Henry II. The Queen and the Duke of Edinburgh were to attend a celebratory service at the cathedral, where my eldest brother Roger was the head chorister – and who tells me that the Queen smiled at him during the service.

The school, which was a choir school attached to the cathedral, was very involved with the celebrations, and the pupils were instructed to line the cloisters, as the Queen was to make her way to the Chapter House before the service, where she was to be introduced to the dignitaries and the great and good of the City of Gloucester.

As the youngest pupil I was first in the line-up and was really looking forward to meeting this fairy-tale lady whom I had seen on television two years earlier.

Imagine my disappointment when a very smartly dressed lady and gentleman appeared in front of me. The headmaster, Tom Brown, introduced me and I promptly turned my back on her.

"That's not the Queen," I said in a very disappointed voice. "She hasn't got a crown on, so she can't be the Queen!!"

I doubt that she remembered this rather embarrassing incident and, if she did, she wouldn't relate it to an ageing councillor in the Borough of Poole. However, I was ready to apologise if need be!

Going back to my lunch date at the Lighthouse, I was now in another line-up. She didn't stop to talk but merely shook hands with me and carried out a very brief conversation with Judy, the contents of which I cannot recall. At the time I didn't realise that I was to see her three more times at various garden parties at Buckingham Palace. I also mentioned her at every citizenship ceremony that I attended in later years as Sheriff of Poole. She had confirmed that Poole could retain the office of sheriff, after local government reorganisation in the seventies, and had given a charter to the borough confirming this, the charter originally granted by Elizabeth I. Interestingly, Poole is one of only fifteen towns and cities that still exercises the right to have a sheriff, and I am still involved with the National Association of City and Town Sheriffs of England and Wales, and travel every year to a convention at one of the fifteen venues.

After the reopening of the Lighthouse, the royal party left the building and proceeded to the royal limousine to be taken to the RNLI headquarters. The mayor, who wished her well on her departure, later told me that the duke had glanced into the royal Bentley and, seeing the huge array of flowers that covered much of the floor, was heard to say, "Looks like a ruddy funeral car in there."

I don't doubt that, as it did look remarkably like some sort of funeral car; and I wonder to this day what happens to the thousands of flowers that are presented to Her Majesty almost on a daily basis.

We wished Her Majesty and His Royal Highness a timely goodbye and moved on to consume the remainder of the feast that we had been enjoying prior to the royal arrival.

20th June 2005

Lead us not into temptation

Today is Wednesday and, as usual for this day of the week, I have been to visit Albert at his lovely home in the village of West Moors in Dorset. Albert suffers from Parkinson's disease, an affliction that he has borne bravely for over twenty years.

I had seen him decline over the short time that I had known him as the symptoms of this awful disease increased in severity.

I have a huge degree of respect for Albert and the way in which both he and his charming wife Susan have coped with his crippling ailment. He has no time for sympathy and has spurned most offers of material help, feeling that it would be an admission that his illness had got the better of him. He still sleeps upstairs; and he doesn't see the need of a stair lift whilst he can still manage the stairs. The fact that every ascent and descent takes the best part of twenty minutes, each fraught with danger, means nothing to him.

Albert and I usually watch Prime Minister's Question Time on my Wednesday visits, arguing about various political points, and then set about playing a few games of cards, using buttons as gambling money. The rules of my care organisation expressly forbid the practice of gambling with real money and, whilst he was a gambler of some years' experience, he accepted that he was not going to be able to deprive me of my hard-earned cash. We would have great fun together, winning and losing buttons, whilst Susan attended her weekly arts course.

Today, Albert seemed to be particularly pleased with himself and decided that, rather than play cards, he would just like to sit and talk, reminiscing over a very eventful and colourful past. We took tea together and then wandered around the garden, enjoying the heat of the summer sun. As I was about to leave, he reached for his wallet and then proceeded to offer me a crisp new £20 note with the words:

"Please accept this for all you have done for me over the past few months."

Embarrassed, I replied, "Sorry Albert, it is the policy of our organisation not to accept any tips or offers of financial reward."

I was deeply aware that acceptance of such an offer would constitute a grave breach of contract, which could lead to a two-tier service, the better care being offered to those who gave the largest amount.

He was obviously very hurt by my refusal. I tried to reason with him and assured him that if he donated the money directly to the organisation, it would be gratefully received and faithfully applied. Realising eventually that I wasn't going to accept the money, he then offered me a drink of cool beer, but once again I had to refuse as the consumption of alcohol was strictly off limits in clients' homes. This refusal was easier, as I was able to point out that I had to drive and would therefore not touch a drop.

On leaving him that afternoon, I got the distinct impression that the friendship we had developed over the months had taken a severe knock. I had, through regulations, become an employee of a care organisation rather than a friend. He had lost sight of the simple fact that I was being paid to visit him and that, whilst I wanted to remain his friend, I had to observe certain rules that were not always consistent with the usual meaning of friendship.

Drinking on duty was strictly forbidden, and the afternoon with Albert served to remind me that we mustn't let our emotions rule our heads and that we must remain totally professional.

Similar situations had occurred before, and I well remember the morning with Ralph Pembleton-Smythe last year and his words: "Rules are there to be broken." How wrong he was.

24th July 2005

Risk assessment and a pot of aqueous cream BP

During training undertaken by care assistants, great emphasis is placed on the subject of risk assessment and health and safety, involving both the student and the future client. The subject of risk assessment takes up an entire day of lecturing and testing, and I was particularly interested in it, as I had made a study of the subject in my previous employment and in my roles as a school governor, trustee of youth organisations and local councillor. In short, we were warned that any action would be followed by an inevitable consequence, and that such a consequence would be either beneficial or carry some element of risk. We were told that we should assess such risks and carry out our duties accordingly, as risks invariably involve hazards; and it was also our duty to identify and remove any hazards before we went about our daily work. This is not rocket science; but in the hands of the inexperienced and less well-educated folk among us, it failed to point out the golden rule – whatever hadn't been foreseen *will* happen, and sooner rather than later.

With this in mind, I felt supremely confident as I set off today for a new assignment of personal care, having been informed that I had to be proficient in this aspect of care before I could gain my National Vocational Qualification (NVQ) Stage 2. This was to be a regular and relatively simple task of getting someone up in the morning and assisting in all of the necessary aspects of getting out of bed and making them ready for the forthcoming day. It meant, in short, helping with all of the things that everyone had to do first thing in the morning: using the toilet, washing, shaving, showering, dressing and feeding, etc. Nothing could be simpler. This was going to be a piece of cake. Easy flipping peasy.

I arrived at the allotted time of 7.30am, which I thought was a rather early start. Whoever wants to get up at that time of the morning, particularly when they are retired? Despite the early hour, I walked confidently up the long drive, armed with my water thermometer, latex gloves, plastic apron, report sheet and client details. I even had my own hand towel and anti-bacterial handwash. Nora, the client's wife, opened the door and warned me that David was a little unsteady on his feet and not able to do much to help as he was suffering from Parkinson's disease. I would find towels on the radiator and a change of clothing by the bed. She continued:

"Oh! Please don't forget to wipe around the toilet, washbasin and shower. Oh!! If necessary there are clean sheets in the cupboard. Oh!!! Please remember that David is ex-RAF Bomber Command, very proud and doesn't really want you here at all.

"Oh!!!! And he has a rash all over his legs and bottom that requires a liberal application of aqueous cream BP."

With these instructions ringing in my head, I made my way to the small downstairs bedroom with en-suite facilities, to be greeted with the sight of a very forlorn-looking man, sitting amongst his bedding and clothes on the end of a very dishevelled bed. He was short in stature but very distinguished-looking and appeared so desperately unhappy that my first reaction was to give him a big hug and a kiss. However, my professionalism took over and I greeted him with a cheery:

"Hello, I'm Chris, your newly appointed manservant, come to make sure all is in tip-top order. Crewman Chris reporting for duty, SIR!"

He broke into a smile, stood up and immediately fell over onto the floor. That was one risk for which I hadn't bargained, and I went immediately to his aid, remembering just in time from my recent training that it was wrong to try and pick up a client from the floor. My instinct told me to help the poor man; my training told me to dial 999. The first rule of health and safety was to assess the risk to both his body and my own poor old back. I decided to fetch his wife.

We both re-entered the room to find him sitting forlornly on the bed, just as he had done before. With the problem seemingly solved, I dispatched his wife and continued to assess the situation. I looked at the en-suite facilities to see whether there was any unusual risk attached, and was a little dismayed by what I found. To say that the facilities were cramped would be an understatement. At first glance, it appeared that someone could sit on the toilet whilst showering their legs and feet, and clean their teeth at the sink, all at the same time, without too much effort or movement. Coupled with this was the fact that the floor was covered with loose bits of rug, and the only spare wall space was fitted with a very hot radiator. I was glad of my training in risk analysis, which enabled me to see the hazards very clearly. The extra risk was the addition of a client; and a seventeen-stone care assistant and a large tub of aqueous cream BP added to the equation. I was also acutely aware that somehow I was going to have to install a chair somewhere in this very restricted place, as it was clear that David wasn't able to stand-alone for any more than one half of one second!

I donned my apron, pulled on my trusty surgical gloves and proceeded to relieve David of his pyjamas. I then avoided the very hot radiator and edged him towards the shower, the temperature of which I had taken the precaution of noting previously. Before removing his underwear I tested the water again. Scalding hot! Someone was running a cold tap somewhere else in the building! I led David back to the bed and sat him down once again. He looked somewhat confused as I searched for the culprit of the cold water use who, having been located and spoken to, enabled us to make our way back to the shower, when I suddenly realised that I still hadn't found a chair for David to sit on. Back to the bed, and yet more confusion as I searched for a perch.

At last, all was ready, and we both enjoyed an invigorating shower, he naked and me fully clothed. I obviously had to work on my technique, as I felt sure that I wasn't supposed to end up dripping wet, and it was clear that the plastic apron did little to prevent a drenching. It seemed that whenever he got hold of the showerhead, the jet got directed at me. The next problem was how to dry him whilst he was sitting in a very confined place and I was trying to find a dry piece of towel. It is at times like these that one realises that training alone can never cover all eventualities.

Having got him reasonably dry, I removed him from the shower, safely manoeuvred him past the hot radiator and sat him on a small chair in front of the sink and mirror. We continued to dry ourselves, and I somehow managed to cover his nakedness with a clean vest. Then, crouching somewhat uncomfortably, wedged between the sink and the toilet bowl, I applied liberal dollops of aqueous cream BP to his legs, feet and bottom. Placing the pot of cream on the closed toilet seat, I then proceeded to fill the basin with hot water for the next task – shaving. Happy in my work, having successfully negotiated the shower, I succeeded in creating a fine amount of soapy suds from an ancient shaving brush and stick with which I had been provided. It struck me as odd that a person with so many deep wrinkles and such an obvious tendency to grow a dense beard overnight still relied on a wet shave when an electric razor would be far safer.

However, as I contemplated the task ahead and the enormity of the risk involved in the use of an exceedingly sharp object so close to the jugular vein, I was somewhat relieved to realise that David was keen to do the shaving job himself. My recollection of the events that followed his grab for the shaving brush will remain forever etched on my memory as a nightmare being played before me in slow motion.

As this frail, elderly gentleman moved forwards to grasp the brush, he involuntarily moved his small pink and naked foot to within a whisker of my size ten Clarks' stout walking boots that I found so comfortable to work in. Aware that seventeen-plus stone was about to fall upon these delicate little pinkies with the inevitable breaking of brittle bones, I made a quick movement away from the risk. This seemingly slight action brought forth vivid, but distant, memories of science lessons, which had repeatedly taught me a strange theory of immovable objects being met by immovable forces. To say that a situation of mammoth proportions was about to be unleashed is an understatement.

As I moved backwards, it became evident that the toilet was going to prevent movement away from the ensuing maelstrom from hell. The shaving brush left my right hand like a rocket and stuck momentarily on the ceiling, whilst the soaking wet flannel in my left hand flew wetly onto the face of my client. One of my legs caught under the chair and caused it to wobble and topple over in the direction of the bedroom, taking client and flannel with it, whilst the other leg went I know not where, as the shaving brush fell onto my head. I suppose it was inevitable that I was going to fall, but how could I be so unlucky as to fall in the way that I did, onto the toilet lid, with my bum placed neatly amongst the now shattered pot of aqueous cream BP.

Having frequently mused over the meaning of the initials BP, I was now fully aware of their significance. Bum Problem!

The noise of this little escapade had not gone unnoticed by the rest of the household, and as I was trying to scrape this ghastly cream from my bottom I became aware that I had an audience. I don't know how many people have sat in a pot of cream before, but let me warn everyone against such a practice. The stuff, which is so good on rashes, yet has no smell but looks like Brylcreem, can get into places that you didn't know existed when used the wrong way. Clearly the use of it as a landing cushion is not to be recommended.

I have to admit that the aftermath of this incident was one of the lowest points of my new career as a care worker. Having taken one and a half hours to rectify the mess that had been created, I realised that it was a good job I only had one personal care visit to make that morning. Any more like that and I was likely to use a whole day on two simple tasks. I was acutely aware that I was going to get a somewhat unfavourable response to my written report to the office on the incident, and that a serious complaint was likely from the family concerned. It could easily be an untimely end to a short-lived career. Aqueous cream remained with me for the rest of the day and for some time afterwards. I was relieved to get back home where I could divest myself of the offending trousers whilst I perused the situations vacant column of the local paper. At least I was going to be saved from the ordeal of taking my NVQ.

P.S. As the days passed and turned into weeks, it became increasingly obvious that I was not going to be the subject of disciplinary action and that David's wife had not lodged a complaint. I am very happy to report that, to date, I still visit David every morning and that we now fully understand each other. He suffered no physical damage and, after my apologies and explanation, we now fully understand each other. I put the cream away immediately after use and he foams his own shaving brush whilst keeping his feet very carefully under his chair. After the necessary ablutions, we go for a short walk together and chat about nothing in particular.

28th July 2005
Don't call the fire brigade!

I can't believe it possible that I could be faced with a health and safety situation just four days from my previous near disaster. I have learned very quickly to take one day at a time, as a care worker should never assume that any day, however carefully mapped out for them by their line manager, will proceed according to plan. It is strange how the most mundane of tasks can blow up into a situation of mammoth proportions. Simple tasks like putting a client to bed that usually take no more than half an hour can end up causing a rippling effect that means continuing work into the small hours whilst neglecting other clients who desperately need help.

This evening has caused ripples that have come close to bringing down the entire network of our care workers for a whole evening. It seemed a simple enough task, but my stupidity in trying to do a task myself that demanded two carers led to a bizarre situation that, had I waited for assistance, would never have occurred. However, I must say that the experience brought me much closer to understanding the work of the emergency services. This was particularly relevant, as in my spare time I sit on the County Fire Authority as an elected member and am frequently questioning the item on the agenda which reads, 'False alarms with good intent'! However can anyone knowingly make a false alarm?

Imagine, if you can, a typical balmy July evening, where thunderstorms are threatened throughout the night.

The breeze outside had freshened to a very strong wind as the first sign of rain for some weeks began to splash on the windscreen while I rushed from job to job, trying to put my evening clients to bed and reassure them that all would be well until morning, when I would get them up again. By 10pm I was getting both very wet and extremely tired. I had an almost guilty feeling of relief as I stopped my car outside the house of my last client, who had such needs that it required the presence of two care workers.

Clarissa is a very special lady who everyone loves to help. It was most unusual for male care workers to administer personal care to female clients, and in fact in my present employment it is usually not encouraged. It seems that male carers were somehow viewed as sexual predators.

However, Clarissa insisted that she had none but male carers, and I always assumed that this was because her physical disabilities made her feel particularly vulnerable and she felt more assured by the presence of male carers.

Whatever the reason, she had been happily married, though now sadly widowed, and had a very supportive family of three sons, three daughters-in-law and countless grandchildren. The one attribute that made Clarissa so popular with the staff was her unstoppable and incredible sense of humour and fun. This was despite her weak heart, osteoporosis, arthritis, diabetes and the fact that she had recently had one leg amputated above the knee, which had resulted from a serious ulceration that had turned gangrenous. Her other leg was under threat, but she didn't seem to have a care in the world.

In view of her disabilities, Clarissa had to rely totally on her care workers to get her up in the morning and put her to bed at night, which involved the use of mechanical hoists to get her from one situation to another. In the morning she was given a thorough bed bath, hoisted from the bed to a wheelchair and placed by another hoist onto the toilet. From thence she was hoisted onto a motorised wheelchair where she would happily spend the rest of the day, being totally independent and preparing her own meals from what she called her 'electric chariot'.

At night, the care workers would return to reverse the process and put her back to bed, where she would lie, often awake, until the next morning.

I was to administer personal care with Paul. I arrived first and found Clarissa a little agitated and sitting, as usual, in front of the television, waiting to see the headlines on *News At Ten* before she was whisked away to her bed. I often sat with her until the second carer arrived, but on this occasion she wanted to go to bed right away, complaining that the lights and the television were flickering as a result of the storm outside. She insisted that she wanted to go to the safety of her bed.

It was now almost ten fifteen at night and I was getting a little concerned that Paul had been delayed at his last client. I phoned our emergency number to inform them that I was on my own and was told to do what I could until help arrived. I was told that Paul and myself were the only carers still at work. I took Clarissa into the bathroom, where we managed to wash, and I attached a night bag to her catheter arrangement. I then took her into the bedroom where, totally against all reason and common sense, I proceeded to fix the sling around her to enable us to hoist her from her chariot onto the bed. Two carers, for health and safety reasons, should undertake this operation, although I sometimes had to do the task myself. It was now 10.30pm and still no sign of Paul. I phoned the office again, only to be told to be patient and that help was on its way.

It was at this point that the situation took on an altogether surreal turn, as if I were watching from the outside and all the actions were being played out before me as if in a dream. Clarissa was adamant that, having secured the sling, I could hoist her by myself into her welcoming bed, and she insisted that I tried to do so. I reluctantly fixed the sling to the hoist and pressed the up button. I was very relieved to see Clarissa rising above me, seemingly happy with the situation. When she reached the desired height, I pressed the button for sideways movement – and it was at this point that things started to go horribly wrong.

The storm outside had increased to a very severe gale that was obviously affecting the continuity of the electricity supply. The lights flickered dangerously and then failed altogether as we experienced a power cut.

Poor Clarissa, jolted by the sudden lack of power, swung from side to side like some distorted pendulum suspended from an invisible clock in a Hans Christian Andersen story. I searched for a torch in the darkness and, just as I found it and switched it on, the power returned. As I looked up at Clarissa I saw her face beaming with humour, as she had obviously seen the funny side of a potentially dreadful situation. She also saw the look of abject panic on my face as I made straight for the button and tried to get her over to her night-time refuge. There then came a crash of deafening thunder and an unbelievably bright flash of lightning, which signified that the storm was right overhead.

There was a noise that could only be described as a loud ***phutt***, together with a flash and puff of blue smoke from the hoist's electric motor as it failed to do as it was told. I assumed that a lightning strike had knocked out the motor with a power surge. Despite frantic pressing of buttons, I could do nothing to make the damned thing work. The hoist was also too high to try to operate manually. Now I was in an impossible situation. Clarissa was well clear of the wheelchair and about two feet sideways from, and five feet above, the bed, her head about six inches from the ceiling. I really wished that she had thought what to do next. She came up with the most ridiculous suggestion. "Why not make us both a nice cup of tea?" Which is precisely what I did, ending up in the most surreal of situations, clambering onto a chair to hand my client a steaming hot cup of tea, whilst she swung several feet from the floor. How was I going to explain this to my line manager?

Paul arrived and laughed. Clarissa nodded knowingly and laughed as well and asked Paul if he would like a cup of tea. I phoned the office and the on-call member of staff, once he had got over my original explanation, laughed as well. I asked him sarcastically if he would like to join us for a cup of tea, and he answered that he might well join us as he had never come across such a situation before. With no evident way out of my present conundrum, I thanked the member of staff for his obvious concern and slammed the phone down.

The doorbell rang and I found two more care workers on the doorstep, having been called out from their cosy homes for this emergency situation to see if they could help. News of this situation was spreading like wildfire. Tea was made for the new arrivals, who joined us in the bedroom to give much advice and cause yet more laughter. Clarissa continued to swing from the ceiling, a wicked grin on her face.

Then I had a brainwave. Clarissa was clearly in a very hazardous position, which was not going to improve by leaving her there for much longer. Remembering my health and safety at work procedures and my risk assessment manuals, I decided that it would put staff at risk to attempt to try and get Clarissa down without the correct equipment. It would also mean a considerable risk to her, as she was unable to help much and a fall from a great height could prove fatal, not only to her but also to the poor unfortunate soul upon whom she might fall. I was going to use all of my training to call the paramedics, and pass the buck.

I dialled 999 and explained that, whilst this was not an acute emergency, a fairly speedy response would be appreciated, in view of the psychological danger to my client. The ambulance, which must have been waiting round the corner, arrived almost immediately, blue lights flashing and sirens wailing, followed almost as quickly by a paramedic rapid response vehicle, also with siren sounding and lights flashing. This, having successfully woken up the entire neighbourhood, caused an influx of worried neighbours who were always concerned for the welfare of the ever happy and very popular Clarissa.

We had now delegated one of the care workers to the sole task of preparing tea for the many people who were now crowding into her small bungalow, whilst Clarissa continued to sway from side to side. The ambulance crew acted with their usual professionalism, in that they somehow managed to commandeer a couple of stepladders, which enabled them to get close to their patient, whilst Clarissa suggested opening a few bottles of wine to help the party "go with a swing!" Then I noticed a couple of policemen who had come to see what all the fuss was about. They suggested that the fire brigade might well help with the on-going incident.

"No! Don't call the fire brigade," I pleaded, knowing that I would be a laughing stock at the next Fire Authority meeting. I now fully understood the meaning of a false alarm with good intent.

There were now so many people in the bungalow that I needed to get outside to regain my composure and think about what to do next. Paul arrived at my side and said:

"Don't worry. The ambulance crew has brought her down using the manual key. Everything's fine – except that there seems to be a lot of cups and glasses to wash up!"

I noticed that people were beginning to leave, and soon the street was back to its peaceful normality. Paul and I made sure that Clarissa was comfortable and that all was well and then left the scene to retire to home and then to bed.

Thankfully, Clarissa phoned the office the next day to explain that the entire situation was her fault as she had insisted that I try to hoist her on my own, and that the storm had caused the hoist breakdown. However, as this was a serious incident and had to be reported to the relevant authorities, I was, quite rightly, called to appear before a disciplinary hearing. The hearing date duly arrived and found against me. However, because of the mitigating circumstances, I was only given a first written warning that would remain on my file for one year. It did give me some understanding of the process, and I found myself, as a staff association representative, helping others at local hearings.

And Clarissa? She still chuckles at the whole episode and is still her usual cheery self. The only downside for her was having to stay in bed until the hoist was repaired. I continued to visit her, but made sure I did nothing in the way of care until the second carer arrived.

21st August 2005
A man of courage

Today I have made my first visit to Donald since he returned from hospital, having undergone another replacement hip operation. I have been giving personal care to Don for over a year and have become quite close to the old war hero. Until this time, his arthritic joints had made him fairly immobile and I'd had to administer quite comprehensive care. It must have been a huge relief for him to have had just one part of his body fixed, so as to enable it to function reasonably well, after so much suffering. The reason for my visit was to re-start his care package and to assist in a risk assessment of his new situation. This would, hopefully, enable me to move him around safely in the future without any danger to him or myself.

Don had told me some time ago that his arthritis problems could be traced back to the Second World War, when he had been a fighter pilot. Based in Northern England, he had engaged enemy war planes in one particular dog fight, shot down a couple of them and, having run out of ammunition and being very low on fuel, was returning to base when he noticed an enemy bomber heading for a major city. Desperate to stop the potential carnage of the city's population, he deliberately aimed his plane at the bomber and crashed into its wing, causing it to plummet onto open farmland. He bailed out and landed with such force that he sustained a broken knee, hip and numerous other fractures but was otherwise safe and sound.

Shortly afterwards, and before he had properly healed, he made his limping way south to help the RAF in their desperate struggle to fend off the threatened German invasion. He was soon back in the air and was shot down midway across the English Channel following a determined dogfight, where he had downed enemy planes. Again he bailed out, this time into the sea, and swam eight miles back to England to re-join his squadron.

This time the injuries and extreme damp did untold damage to his joints, and ever since he has suffered from ever worsening mobility problems. It is a real privilege to know this man and to be able to help him, though he always insists that he really doesn't need any help at all.

I quickly assessed that he was going to need even more care than before his first hip replacement. It seemed so unfair that a man of such courage had to undergo so much suffering. I assured him that I would continue to care for him. For which he expressed his gratitude, whilst pointing out that he didn't really need any help but that he was pleased that I would be seeing him every day and would be glad of the company.

My visit to Don served to remind me of my health and safety obligations to all my clients. After a change of circumstances, would I be able to carry out the same degree of care without implementing a new risk assessment, which might involve extra equipment or possibly the help of another carer?

As someone who had the good fortune to be born after the war, but close enough to remember the severe bomb damage around London and to experience the rationing that was still in force in my youth, it was really humbling to meet people such as Don who had put country and freedom above his own life and performed such unrecognised heroics for his fellow countrymen.

I often come across people who are so dismissive of their own achievements that they keep their experiences close to their chest and never boast about what they have achieved. My on-going battle to get George to open up to me was one of these instances, and I look forward to my next visit when I am determined to find out why he is so insular and difficult to communicate with.

4th September 2005
George and the doughnuts

I have just spent another two hours with George and have uncovered yet another revelation about his interesting past. Having gained his trust after many fruitless visits, during which I had started to become another subject for his wife's persistent nagging, I was beginning to understand the man himself and was beginning to form quite a strong bond of friendship. It would be wrong for me to relate on paper the job that he used to have, as this might easily identify him. Suffice it to say that it involved both government at the highest level and the royal household. He related to me many interesting stories of his life before his retirement, on the strict understanding that I kept all of them secret.

In order to get him to open up, I needed to remove him from a very depressing home situation and get him interested in life again. Today is the first day that I have arrived to find him ready and waiting to go out.

"Please could we try somewhere different today?" he pleaded. "I'm a little tired of going to the beach every week."

"Of course we can," I replied, rather grateful that I could escape the tourist traffic.

We made our way to the New Forest, in search of a nice tearoom, which we duly found. It is quite a pleasurable part of my work that I have to spend so much time in tearooms, cafes and ice cream parlours, all at someone else's expense. This afternoon we decided to try their homemade doughnuts and enjoyed them so much that we made a pact that we would try doughnuts at as many local eateries as we could and then make a list of their respective quality, perhaps compiling the ultimate guide to 'Dorset Doughnuts'. As I was licking the last remnants of sugar and raspberry jam from my sticky fingers I thought of the many times that I had found myself consuming rich gooey food, simply in the pursuit of my chosen career. This was becoming a very enjoyable job, but one that was doing absolutely nothing to slim my ample girth.

It was to transpire, after much doughnut consumption, that George had picked the overall winner so far. We still had dozens of eateries to test but, rather than a doughnut, he had chosen a rum baba, with loads of syrup and oodles of cream, as his favourite teatime delicacy, so the doughnut project was wasted as we pursued the best rum baba.

Whilst he was consuming his second doughnut I remembered the many teas that had been laid out for my clients and myself by their partners so that we could enjoy food during the respite hours. These teas usually comprised home-baked cakes, bread and scones and homemade jams. It was whilst pondering these delicacies that the fond memory of the hours I had spent last year with a retired vicar came to mind.

1st August 2004
Tea with the vicar

Now that I am trained and experienced in most disabilities and eccentricities, this particular day in my life will remain etched in my mind for many years as one for which I was totally unprepared. It involves a deaf reverend gentleman of considerable age, with an encyclopaedic knowledge of all things biblical, particularly the Book of Job. His name was the Reverend Walter Waters. His address – The Old Rectory, Piddlehideme (name changed for obvious reasons) Dorset – seemed particularly fitting to his obvious vocation. The age attributed to him on my client details put him very well past retirement and very close to the age that qualifies for a personal message from the Queen. I assumed that, after retirement, he had somehow managed to maintain his 'living' in such a way as to allow him to remain in the house that at one time went with his parish responsibilities.

I was intrigued by my instructions that read: *Walter is quite deaf but refuses to wear any auditory aids. He lives in a very large home with a faithful and longstanding housekeeper, who occasionally needs to leave him alone whilst she attends to the shopping needs of the household.* It seemed that it was no longer possible to leave poor Walter alone for any appreciable amount of time, as his arthritis had made it difficult for him to perform any functions that required movement, without some degree of help. His mental capacity was superb for his age of ninety-eight years, but his body was weak and his hearing difficulties were not helped by his refusal to wear a hearing aid. The details specifically stated that Walter, once prompted, would talk for hours on the Book of Job, and he would take little notice of time, once immersed in his favourite subject. In short, conversation would be rather one-sided.

I felt particularly qualified to undertake this assignment, as I had received much training in my youth on all things ecclesiastical. I had, at the early age of eight years old, become a chorister at Gloucester Cathedral. This meant that I had to attend cathedral services on a very regular basis, where I duly sang like an angel and sat through so many lessons and sermons that I became, for a boy of such tender years, quite an expert on the Bible.

When my voice broke with the inevitable onset of puberty, I found that it not only lowered my voice but also lowered a couple of other attributes of young males to a very noticeable degree. This supposedly matured me; so, after that maturity, together with the loss of voice, I was man enough to become a 'server'. This meant helping reverend gentlemen during the discharge of morning communion. This was a very grown-up task that involved, on occasions, taking breakfast with a succession of canons, deacons, archdeacons, deans and bishops, which invariably involved in-depth discussions on all things religious and heavenly.

This early life training gave me a distinct advantage when dealing with men of the cloth, in that I understood them and had actually lived within their very closed environment. They were a world apart from real life, in that rarely did the clergyman's wife cook breakfast in the privileged environment of the cathedral close and its precincts. There was invariably a housekeeper who managed the day-to-day lives of these rather superior clergy.

It was with these thoughts of my childhood in my mind that I made my way up the long gravel path that led to the rectory. I instinctively knew that the door was going to be answered by a faithful housekeeper and that I was about to meet a kind elderly gentleman who lived in the distant past, without any idea of the modern world. Shortly after I heard the sound of the bell, that was connected to a great pull cord that hung by the front door, the door was opened by the most 'housekeeperish' looking lady I have ever encountered. She wore a sensible grey plaid skirt and a freshly laundered white blouse beneath a very expensive-looking grey woollen cardigan. Her grey hair was pulled back into a tight and austere-looking bun which, together with her highly sensible grey court shoes, made her the picture of household authority.

"I am Chris from the care organisation. I have an appointment with the Reverend Walter Waters." I felt that this lady deserved the most complete introduction.

"The Reverend is expecting you. Please follow me. He is in the library."

I duly followed along a corridor whose length would have done a medium-sized hotel proud. I passed many doors, all crafted from the most beautifully carved mahogany. The gentle and mesmerising tick… tock… of a large grandfather clock was the only sound, apart from that of our footsteps on the highly polished floor. Miss Housekeeper neither spoke nor needed to, as she obviously knew both her and my place and proceeded with absolute authority. On entering the library she announced:

"Reverend Waters, Mr Christopher Bulteel is here from the care agency and he wishes to spend a little time with you whilst I go about the duties of the household. Tea is laid out in the garden room. Mr Bulteel will brew the tea."

"Thank you, Mimi my dear, that will be all until supper time."

With those few words Mimi retired from the room and left me alone with this larger than life character. I stood there for some time, waiting for a reaction from the ecclesiastical gentleman who sat at the opposite end of the room in front of a welcoming log fire. As I stood patiently, waiting for some sort of invitation to proceed further, I took stock of my surroundings. Every wall was fitted from floor to ceiling with bookshelves that contained books of every size and description. There seemed to be no definite order or system in arrangement, paperbacks sharing the same space as expensive-looking leather-bound tomes. However, all looked very well used, and I felt sure that every book in this considerable collection had actually been read. In the centre of the room stood a huge round table, on which were spread hundreds of pages of typed manuscript, almost covering a small ancient typewriter.

A few books lay open, giving the impression that someone had recently left the table for a short respite from deep research. Two leather chairs were placed in front of the fire, one of which was occupied by Walter. It did strike me as odd that there was a fire alight in August, but it was a little chilly in this ancient rectory and people of advancing years often felt the cold, even when it was really quite warm. Walter beckoned me to join him by pointing to the vacant chair.

As I took my place beside him I became aware of the huge character etched onto his face. The wrinkles betrayed great age, the eyes gave hints of great wisdom and he sported a full white beard that seemed slightly stained around the mouth. It soon became clear that he had an unfortunate twitch of the head that occurred whenever he was about to move any part of his body. This might account for the slight staining, as it was obvious that whenever he tried to put anything into his mouth, a twitch would ensue that would leave particles of food hanging in his beard. Any attempt to retrieve these lost morsels with his tongue would create another twitch that would embed the food even deeper. I sat in the vacant chair and introduced myself.

"Hello Reverend Waters, I'm Chris from the care agency."

"How nice to see you," he replied, with an obvious defect of speech. It appeared that he was unable to pronounce the letter 's' without adding an 'h' to it, making every 's' last longer than it should. For example, instead of saying Chris, he would say Chrish. This was coupled with an obvious problem with swallowing, which meant that every time he used the letter 's' a cloud of fine mist, composed of built-up saliva, would issue forth from his mouth. It quickly became obvious that to have any decent conversation with this man would necessitate sitting downwind. "But please don't call me Reverend Waters. Everyone calls me Joe."

I enquired as to how he had gained the name of Joe.

"In my youth I was particularly interested in the life of Job, the author of the Book of Job. I used to be called Job as a joke, which became lengthened to Holy Job when I started my ecclesiastical training, which then changed to Holy Joe over the years and then to plain Joe."

After a seemingly complete clear-out of saliva, he continued: "But we are not here to talk about me. Do you want to hear about my new work on the life and times of Job, with particular emphasis on his patience and skill as a comforter?"

"I would love to hear more of your work. When I was a boy I got very used to hearing pieces from the Book of Job whilst I listened to lessons and sermons. I used to be a chorister."

"What was that you said?" he enquired. "Forrester did you say... *Forrester*? Were you some kind of lumberjack?"

My mind immediately went into some strange imagined world of a Monty Python sketch concerning lumberjacks and choirboys carrying axes instead of hymnbooks.

"No, Joe… CHORISTER!" I shouted. "I was in the choir!!"

"Oh dear!" he replied. "And was it serious. Did it burn down the whole forest?"

"No, not fire! CHOIR!" I shouted at the top of my voice.

"That's all right, then. Just as well the fire brigade was on hire, although in my young day they were always free. Times change, I suppose."

This was turning into a somewhat difficult afternoon, where I needed to change the subject before the conversation degenerated into an absolute shambles

"How about some tea?!" I bellowed, hoping to be able to escape into the kitchen for a while.

"It's very kind of you to offer to help, but I had a pee shortly before you arrived. Tell you what, though; I could murder a cup of tea. How about it? I believe Mimi left something in the garden room."

I helped him to his feet and we made our way to the garden room, which turned out to be a vast conservatory, furnished with wicker furniture and heated to such a degree that the many tropical plants seemed to flourish in the humid environment despite the cooler weather outside.

A table had been laid with thinly sliced bread and butter, jam and homemade fruitcake. I found the kitchen and brewed a pot of strong tea, using the tin marked 'Earl Grey'. As I poured the first cup of rich brown liquid, Joe started to regale me with all of the relevant facts of his new literary work, to which I gave knowing nods at various points. It was useless to interject as I felt sure that he would mishear what I said and any misunderstanding might offend. It was interesting nonetheless that his speech impediment gradually disappeared as he became more engrossed in his subject.

It became evident that the Reverend Holy Joe Waters was an exceptionally well-educated man who had done much in his life to help other folk less fortunate than himself. He had set up missions all over the globe and had done much to alleviate hunger and suffering in a very cruel world. His talk on the Book of Job soon shifted to his missionary work, and I became aware that I was privileged to be in the presence of a very holy and devout man whose brain was not in any way affected by his great age. I listened to him for over two hours and was entranced by this truly memorable character. I am so grateful that I was able to maintain a lasting friendship with him, during which this ancient and very experienced gentleman taught me much about life and imparted to me a wisdom that would be difficult to find again.

One particular story of his will remain etched in my memory of him as a gentle, sincere man who knew nothing but the truth and whose sense of humour was tickled by the simplest of circumstances that led to great mirth.

One Sunday he was feeling a little depressed that attendance at Holy Communion was slipping. The depression had been going on for most of the preceding week and he felt at a total loss as to how to attract new parishioners to the church. His work on the sermon for the week was greatly impeded by his depressed state and he began to sink into a state of despair. Eventually he made his way to the church and knelt at the altar to pray.

"Please, God, give me inspiration to challenge the village and get them to attend communion."

Feeling slightly easier and comforted by prayer, he made his way to the communion cupboard to take out the wine and wafers to set up the table by the altar. He was horrified to find that all of the wine had gone and all that was left was a silver tray of wafers.

With only half an hour to go to the service he began to panic and wonder how the Good Lord could have let him down so quickly after praying for help. How would he manage to increase his congregation, when those few who actually came appeared to be there for the wine alone, which was singularly lacking for this Sunday! In desperation, he made for the rectory in search of a bottle of red wine. To his horror there was no bottle that looked like wine, and all he could find were various spirits, that he kept to offer to senior clergy when they visited. He didn't partake of alcohol, so didn't have any idea which drink was what.

He picked up a bottle of fine Napoleon brandy, which had five stars and the letters VSOP on the label. As this was a darker liquid than the others, he assumed that it was more likely to be a fortified wine. It wasn't quite red, but he could add a drop of cochineal to make it look more like communion wine. He guessed that the letters VSOP stood for Vineyards Selection Of Perfection, rather than the correct Very Superior Old Pale. Any port in a storm, he thought, as he hurried back to the church, bottle and cochineal hidden beneath his cassock. He carefully emptied the brandy into the chalice and added a single drop of colouring, which produced a perfect copy of communion wine.

As he didn't drink, he didn't taste the liquid. If he had, he might have received a very pleasant surprise. He served his concoction at communion but failed to notice the look of satisfaction on the faces of his flock as he entered into the delivery of his sermon which, incidentally, was about the excesses of life and the need to moderate one's tastes.

He thought nothing more about it, except to begin to doubt the power of prayer, as he hadn't managed to pull in an increased congregation that Sunday. All that I can conclude is that word must have spread throughout the parish about the new communion wine, for when I questioned Joe further about his prayers and his temporary loss of faith, he replied:

"The very next Sunday I was feeling particularly depressed, until I looked up at the communion rail and saw a queue of people stretching down the aisle and outside the church. I don't know to this day how this happened, but my prayers were answered and I was able to deliver a sermon to a vastly increased congregation."

"And what happened thereafter?" I asked.

"Well, nothing really. The congregation continued to grow, and I kept on topping up the communion wine with that new wine that came from the local off-licence. The power of prayer is a truly wonderful thing!"

I couldn't help wondering what went through Mimi's mind when she looked at the requests for church purchases from Joe, to add to the weekly shopping list. She must have wondered what Joe was doing on his visits to the church vestry but chose to remain silent as she believed that a man of Joe's great age deserved some treats and comforts in life.

12th September 2006

The legacy of an addiction

Today could not be classed as an exceptional day, as I visit Colin every morning and assist him in the mundane task of getting himself ready to face the world. I use the word 'mundane' for a repetitive daily task; it is not directed towards Colin, who could never be called mundane. His only problem is his obvious lack of legs, although he seems to make light of his severe disability, telling me on frequent occasions that there are many people worse off than him.

I often wondered at his stoicism and listened in awe as he blamed his disability fairly and squarely on himself. The reaction when I first met him was that he would actually be easier to deal with than most of my clients, as he jokingly said:

"Of course, I shall be able to save you time and money. I do not have legs and feet washed, and have no need for a chiropodist or the expense of socks and shoes!"

Poor Colin was the cause of his own disability, as a recovering alcoholic who had not touched a drop of liquor for over forty years.

However, when he was drinking, he drank for the world and, whenever he couldn't get hold of drink, he drank anything that contained alcohol, whether it was methylated spirits, Old Spice aftershave or home-produced wood alcohol. He would drink himself into oblivion, and the gutter would beckon, until he reached the utter depths of depravity and despair.

However, he gave up alcohol and spent his later years lecturing at meetings of Alcoholics Anonymous, helping many hundreds of people in their battle with the bottle.

His past history of alcohol abuse had caught up with him and caused diabetes and massive problems to his circulatory system. This led to the amputation of his left foot, which in turn gave rise to an infection of a super bug, which caused the onset of gangrene and led to the amputation of his left leg. Then his right leg developed ulcers that failed to heal and again went gangrenous, leading to the inevitable amputation of his right leg. Most people would have been traumatised by such a severe disability, but Colin took it on the chin and continued to look at life in a positive way.

He coped with his lot and continued to help others, and he inspired the many people who came into contact with him. Whenever I came across a lesser disability, where a client complained about his situation, I spoke of Colin, who felt that he was lucky to be alive and to have reached the great age of eighty-four years.

Today, Colin has told me of the great suffering that he has experienced and of the heartache that he caused others during his years under the influence of alcohol. It was a heart-rending tale that he related often to the local Alcoholics Anonymous group and one that had helped very many people.

He is much loved and respected and, despite his difficulties, has achieved so much good in his life that I feel assured that he will gain a much deserved place in heaven when his time eventually comes.

Whenever I speak to Colin, I am reminded of those clients who have not followed his path and who remain slaves to the bottle. The nature of my job means that I tend to come into contact with elderly men, a lot of whom were involved with some kind of military service during the past wars. Sometimes the trauma of their experiences led them to seek solace in alcohol, and a few of those had remained firmly attached to this false comforter.

One such gentleman was Alfred, who I first visited earlier in the year.

18th March 2006
Corned beef and tomatoes

Today I have been called out to an emergency, as Paddy, our resident caring clown, has been taken poorly with a really nasty tummy bug, following a night of celebrating St Patrick's night.

I just knew that this visit would be out of the ordinary, partly because Paddy was given clients who could be both difficult and colourful, and partly because I had been warned that this particular client had an acute drinking problem. I had been instructed to provide Alfred with his lunch and to do anything else that may be required, including his weekly shopping.

I arrived on the stroke of twelve noon at a block of very expensive-looking apartments in one of the more affluent regions of Bournemouth. This was such a posh address that it required the use of an entry phone to get inside the gates, which was duly answered by a concierge, who enquired of me both whom I wished to see and whether I was expected. Having accessed the grounds and parked my car, I was again challenged, on entering the large revolving doors, as to the direction of my visit. Again I was asked whether I was expected, and the client was duly contacted.

"Mr Soames is expecting you. He resides at No 54, which is situated on the fifth floor," said this rather supercilious man in a dark blue uniform with so much gold braid that he looked like the First Sea Lord and Admiral of the Fleet rolled into one. *I* could have told the snooty fool that – and without all the unnecessary carry-on!

"You may use the lifts if you like, rather than taking the stairs."

"Just tell Mr Soames that the care worker is on his way," I replied, wondering why he even thought it necessary to suggest the lift when to use the stairs would require a use of energy and time that I was not prepared to waste. Perhaps care workers were, in some way, likely to contaminate lifts.

I entered the lift and was surprised to find myself reflected in an almost totally mirrored cube. Only the floor had been left without a mirror and was covered instead with an expensive deep shag-piled carpet of a deep purple hue. I pressed the button for Floor 5 and, as the doors closed, wondered what it would be like to commit some immoral act in such an erotic environment. No sooner had the image appeared than I arrived at the destination and noted in my mind a reason for not committing such an act. Not enough time!

As the doors slid open I became aware of the vast size of the apartments. The corridor would have lost my entire home, and it was clear that the fifth floor contained only four flats, each of which must have been huge. I turned left, following the arrows to No 54, walking on the same deep-pile purple carpet, to an open front door. I entered and called out my name.

"Hello, it's Chris from the care organisation. Anyone at home?"

Silly question, really, as it was quite obvious that someone must be at home. There was no response, so I tiptoed forwards, half afraid that I might be in the wrong flat.

A strong smell of exotic tobacco pervaded the atmosphere, and I followed the scent to what was obviously the lounge, where an unforgettable sight met me. Sat in a huge chair, surrounded by tables of various sizes, was what could only be described as a very large man. He was not fat, just huge in proportions, rather like a fairy-tale giant. The tables were strewn with cans of beer and a large variety of pipes, some filled with smouldering tobacco, some obviously awaiting attention. He was pulling on a gargantuan Sherlock Holmes type of pipe and exhaling vast quantities of smoke.

"Hello Chris," he said in greeting. "Pull up a chair and join me in a can."

"Thanks, but I would rather have a cup of tea, if I may," I replied, being aware of our strict rules on alcohol consumption whilst on duty.

"Don't be silly, you boring old fart. Paddy always joins me in a can. Sod the regulations. You are here to care for me, and the care that I need right now is company. Company means beer, which means sharing a can together. You mustn't be such a boring old fart!"

It was the second mention of the words 'boring old fart' that set my mind wondering. I could describe farts with many an adjective, but boring? Never! It is my experience that farts are just about the least boring bodily function that exists. If farts were rated on a Richter scale of one to ten, then number one would be the silent yet devastatingly effective stink bomb of a fart, whilst number ten would be the beans for breakfast, sprouts for lunch, belt and braces, rip your pants and clear the bar type fart. All those in between would be differing in extent but equally effective in relieving boredom, and certainly not creating it.

I well remember such a fart, produced by some mysterious person many years ago. Whilst probably measuring five on the Richter scale, it brought farting to an art form. I was a very young mayor of a small market town at the time, and was attending a church commemoration service in my official capacity, occupying a front pew, adorned with my gold chain of office. I had enjoyed a lavish luncheon, along with most of the congregation, where I had been required to give a speech about the event that we were about to so piously commemorate.

Almost the entire congregation was suffering as I was, with overindulgence of food and alcohol, and we were mostly trying to contain our excess of wind. The church was filled to capacity with the gentlefolk of the county, including the High Sheriff and Lord Lieutenant of Dorset. I felt immensely proud to have reached such a pinnacle of esteem within my community at such a young age. At a point in the service where we were required to change from the kneeling position to a standing one, someone could restrain themselves no longer and let rip a completely unavoidable expulsion of air. It might have gone unnoticed had the organ been playing, but was immediately audible to the entire congregation in such a hushed environment.

What I did next will be a source of shame for the rest of my life. Acting quickly to move blame from myself, although I was totally innocent, I turned purposefully to face the person sitting directly behind me and fixed them with a gaze that implied that I knew the offending sound must have come from them. I was, nonetheless, mortified to find that I was looking into the face of the Lady of the Manor, and horrified that her face had turned bright red, implying guilt.

Many people could not contain their mirth, and the serenity of the occasion degenerated from then on. Now, that fart was certainly not boring and remained the topic of polite conversation at the dinner tables of many a family of the county for months and even years afterwards. If the said lady is reading this now, all I can do is offer my humble apologies and come clean after all these years. However, I digress.

It became quite clear that the presence of an abstinent care worker was not welcomed in this particular home, so I made my way into the kitchen to consult the client file and see what was done on a daily basis to help the person. It seemed that the usual task was to prepare and serve a sandwich, accompanied by a can of liquid refreshment.

I opened the fridge to be confronted with an extraordinary sight. The shelves were crammed with cans of beer and foil-wrapped parcels. I opened up a few of the packages and found round after round of corned beef and tomato sandwiches of varying ages, in varying degrees of consumption and with varying levels of mould contamination. Some had such a growth as to indicate that they had been around for some considerable time. I would have to deal with this very diplomatically, as it was our policy to clear out food only on the instruction of the client, unless it placed them in obvious danger.

I looked further, in search of some sort of sandwich filling, but could only find some fairly fresh and 'in date' sliced corned beef and a plastic bag of tomatoes, together with some 'I can't believe it's not butter' and half a loaf of brown bread. I duly prepared two rounds of sandwich using the only ingredients that I could find and took them into the lounge with a can of the only available liquid, namely a can of Whitbread Best Bitter.

He carefully pulled back the top piece of bread and exclaimed in a booming and very angry and agitated voice:

"Oh no! Not f***ing corned beef again! Have you no imagination? Is there nothing else to eat in this f***ing house? For heaven's sake, take my shopping list and get some decent provisions. Why do they always send such idiots to help me? The list is on the hall table and I've written it myself, so please, please can you do one thing right and return with exactly what is written down on the list? Bring back Paddy, is all I can say."

I was slightly taken aback by this outpouring of bile and explained that I was only trying to do my best in totally strange and difficult circumstances and that I had used the only ingredients available to me.

"Just piss off and do your job!"

I left the room feeling extremely small and dejected, found the shopping list and read it, as follows:

- Whisky – Bottle (litre) Bell's
- Beer – 48 cans
- Lemonade – Bottle (2 litres)
- Tobacco – Lots of Best Balkan
- Ginger (Ale) – (enough to last)
- Matches
- Lighter fuel
- Whisky – (one bottle for spare, can be cheap but not under strength)
- Bread (a loaf of)
- Butter (Can't believe it's not)
- Tomatoes (a few)
- Corned Beef (sliced fresh Tesco's best)
- Aspirins and
- Bog rolls.

So much for variety! I took up the list, together with the accompanying bank notes, and duly did the shopping. Finding him fast asleep on my return, I deposited the goods, left his change and tiptoed out of his flat, never to see him again – assuming that he had instructed my employers that he never wanted anyone but Paddy to visit him in future.

23rd October 2006

Prize giving day

Today I am to visit a world-renowned professor. I say world-renowned a little lightly, as his worldly renown is mainly restricted to those interested in entomology, as this is the field that earned him his degree, doctor's title, and eventually becoming Emeritus Professor in Entomology at a world-famous university. He had retired many years previously but had never given up his quest for knowledge of all things insect, particularly the dung beetle, on which he was a recognised expert.

I had been warned by my client details that he was likely to spend the entire time of my visit regaling me on the life cycle of the dung beetle, whilst I made sure he was safe during the temporary absence of his wife, Mildred, who also possessed a doctorate, although I am unsure in what.

As I knocked on the door of an imposing Victorian townhouse in the centre of Poole, I was becoming increasingly nervous about the task I was due to undertake. I had been chosen to sit with him because it was felt that my life experiences held me in good stead to relate to this formidable character. A most charming lady, who introduced herself as Mildred Mulholland, the wife of Marcus, opened the door. I needed no introduction, as my name badge was clearly visible on my coat lapel.

"Welcome to our humble abode," said Mildred as she beckoned me into an impressive hall. Expertly executed hand-drawn pictures of various beetles adorned the walls, and I noted that a Mildred Mulholland signed all. We continued down the seemingly endless passage to the hub of this learned household, the study-cum-library.

As on previous visits to learned folk, I was impressed with the sheer quantity of books that lined the walls. The customary table in the middle of the room was covered, as is the norm, with many pieces of paper and open books, signifying on-going research. Sat at the table was a most impressive-looking gentleman, who appeared to be immersed in work of the most serious nature. I gave a small, nervous cough to announce my arrival and he looked up from his book and studied me closely over the rim of his half spectacles.

"Ah, you must be Chris. I have been expecting you. I am currently studying the life cycle of the *Onitis aygulus*, representative of a species of dung beetle. A very interesting insect, as I am sure you will agree."

"I'm sorry to disturb you in your very important research. I have been asked to keep you company for a few hours while your wife fulfils various appointments. I must say how impressed I am by your library of impressive books. I would love to look through them."

By this time Mildred had quietly left the scene and I found myself alone with this impressive character.

"Tell me, Christopher, are you interested in books; what have you been reading recently? Do you have a collection of books in your house? I always think that a home without books is a home without a heart. Tell me your most memorable story about your literary past."

"Well, Professor, I do have an unusual tale to tell about my experience with books. It will take a time, but I am sure you will appreciate the outcome."

"Carry on, Chris. And please don't keep calling me professor. The name is Marcus."

"Well, Marcus, I was around eleven years old at the time of this crazy tale. I was a chorister in Gloucester Cathedral and this meant that I was educated at the Cathedral school, namely The King's School, Gloucester.

"Every year the school held a hobbies exhibition and every year I failed to enter, as my hobbies in life were more imaginary than practical. I enjoyed listening to and performing music, reading and writing, and generally being at one with nature by walking for miles through the Cotswold countryside."

"That sounds admirable," replied Marcus, "but how does this fit in with the book theme?"

"Well, I was fed up with not exhibiting in the annual hobbies exhibition," I replied, "and decided to ask my long-suffering mum to help me out, as I really wanted to get involved this year.

"She mentioned food and suggested that I bake a loaf of bread as no one else would have thought of cookery as a hobby and least of all as a later career. I mulled this over and was rewarded with a recipe for bread that seemed quite simple. Mum had told me that I would have to do any baking by myself, with no help from anyone, if I was to win a prize. I asked her about the difference between 'needing' and 'kneading', and she described the difference using old socks rather than dough to demonstrate the way to knead dough. I took the hint."

"And what was the result?" asked Marcus.

"I duly took Mum's advice and diligently followed her recipe for home-baked bread. The result was a surprisingly perfect loaf of bread that smelt like heaven. I duly put the loaf into the exhibition in the morning, accompanied by a dish of butter and homemade jam. I thought nothing more about it until the late afternoon when I was told that I had received first prize for my handiwork!!"

"What an unexpected achievement!" he exclaimed.

"However, the saga doesn't end there," I continued. "The prize giving was to be conducted by none other than Field Marshal, Viscount Montgomery."

Field Marshall Montgomery was a wartime hero who had led the fight against the Germans in many a battle, including fighting against Rommel in the desert. At that time, he was a real war hero and did much to end the horrific Second World War and bring peace to Europe. He really was regarded as a hero, having beaten the enemy on many a military campaign. However, I digress.

I continued to tell him that I was about to receive the book of my choice from this great man and I was looking forward to the great privilege. Most prizewinning boys had chosen books that were likely to impress their teachers or the viscount. There were many items of literature, including books by Marcel Proust, Victor Hugo, and Leo Tolstoy. Books on military strategy featured strongly. Charles Dickens, Shakespeare and Thomas Hardy figured in the English authors, together with various dictionaries, encyclopaedias and technical books related to favourite subjects, but no one had thought of the book that I had chosen for a first prize.

Monty, as he was widely known, asked me, when I was about to receive my book, to step aside so that the audience couldn't hear over the microphone what he was about to tell me. He said that he was delighted to give me the prize and that he doubted that any of the books he had presented so far would actually be read, apart from mine, which he would love to read himself.

The book I had chosen was *Biggles and the Missing Millionaire.*

I returned to reality and Marcus said that he would seek out my book choice and comment at a later date. He continued to regale me with the life story of the dung beetle and came up with a few representative species, such as *Onthophagus taurus*, *Scarabaeus Sacer* and, our favourite, *Onitis aygulus*.

Needless to say, I was in awe of his in-depth knowledge of all things dung beetle, particularly the knowledge that a dung beetle can bury 250 times of dung heavier than itself in one night.

Wow, what a day! But onwards and upwards is what they say!

24th November 2006

A very unexpected send-off

Today I have been to visit Suzanna Simpkins, wife of the late Sam. This is a very special day for me as I have, for the first time, taken on a task that lies outside my usual responsibilities. Sue, as she likes to be called, was married to one of my longest-serving clients, Samuel Simpkins, who was an accountant of some considerable reputation, having practised in the area for most of his working life. Unfortunately, in the twilight of his life he had developed a form of dementia and had suffered a number of minor strokes. However, he had a total and accurate recall of his early life, and I spent many a happy hour in his company.

He had three children, all of whom had been adopted and who worshipped the ground he walked on. He was a truly remarkable man, and my admiration for him was only surpassed by my deep respect for his loving wife who did everything she could to keep her beloved husband at home until the day he died.

I had visited Sam on a weekly basis and often drove him and Sue to Poole Quay, where we would watch boats passing whilst eating enormous ice creams topped with milk flakes. It became the highlight of their week, and I was very sad when Sam passed away, heralding the end of our trips together. However, I had grown so close to this special family that I couldn't take on the usual guidance from my employers, to avoid too much further contact with families once a client had died. The advice was sound, in that the very nature of my job meant that I would lose many clients and could become bogged down with the on-going lives of bereaved families, to the detriment of my own private life.

However, Sam, Sue and family were different, and I simply couldn't break contact, particularly after the huge embarrassment that I suffered after I was invited to Sam's funeral. It is unusual to attend funerals of deceased clients as a major guest; it is usually only as a bystander, to pay one's respects from the back of the church or crematorium. And it is fairly unusual to be invited as a family friend, both to the funeral and the wake afterwards. On this occasion I was especially invited to attend Sam's funeral and the gathering afterwards at a local hotel.

I duly arrived at the allotted time at St Osmond's Church and was very moved by the ceremony and the sincerity of the eulogies to Sam by his three children. The praise by the vicar was equally moving, and told of a lifetime of service to God, family and country. It was with a somewhat elevated heart that I set off for the gathering and wake at the Haven Hotel, where I arrived in fairly good spirits, considering the solemnity of the previous ceremony, feeling that the service had been a celebration of Sam's life, rather than a sad affair.

I was given a very warm welcome at the door by a relative who I had not met before, took a glass of sparkling wine and began to mix with the other guests, somewhat surprised that there seemed to be so many new faces that had been absent from the church. I was extremely grateful to see, at the other end of the room, the familiar face of John, an officer of the local council, who I knew quite well. I made a beeline for him and we spent the next hour deep in conversation about the problems of the local authority. It wasn't until we had finished our rather lavish lunch that I asked him how he knew Sam.

"Sam?" he replied. "Who is Sam?"

"Samuel Simpkins, of course," said I, feeling somewhat bemused.

"And who is Samuel Simpkins? I am not aware that I know anyone of that name."

The conversation was becoming rather surreal.

"Sam, of course. Samuel Simpkins, whose funeral we have just attended and whose life we have just so solemnly celebrated," I continued, feeling a little uneasy as I scanned the room for more familiar faces but failed to see any.

"I don't know whose funeral you have been to, but I have just attended one for Paul White at The Church of The Transfiguration!"

Embarrassment would be too simple a word to describe the utter helplessness that overcame me at that precise moment, as I felt my face getting warmer until it became like a flaming furnace as I coloured to the shade of an overcooked beetroot. I had obviously gone to the wrong hotel and had enjoyed the hospitality of complete strangers. I left by a side door and made for home. On my arrival, there was, inevitably, a message on my answerphone from Sue, asking why I had not been to the Harbour Hotel to meet the extended family. I could only apologise profusely and explain, rather unconvincingly, that I was so overwhelmed by the occasion that I didn't feel I could make it to the hotel. I did, however, promise to visit next Friday as usual and take her to the quayside for our weekly ice cream.

Which brings me to the current day and the reason for staying with this family. Sue is a wonderful person, who has met her sad loss head-on and intends to continue her socialising, which includes bridge drives and games of Scrabble with the local gentlefolk. Her skill at Scrabble is legendary, and whenever I play a game with her I am reminded of a day last year, when I visited two other ladies of the parish, namely Daisy and Edith.

4th April 2005

Bad words do not good friends make!

As I progressed in my career as a care worker I found myself being offered more diverse and interesting work. I was still being given the usual caring tasks, but I was now becoming involved in ever more unusual and responsible tasks that often meant meeting people of rich character, who needed not necessarily care, but a lasting and loyal companionship.

Two such people that I came to know extremely well were Daisy and Edith, two sisters of greatly advanced age who seemed locked in a more serene and genteel era that flew in the face of the fast and stressful 21st century. I don't know to this day who was the elder, as both vied for the privilege of being born before the other. I was only aware that both had begun life soon after the death of Queen Victoria, which meant that they must have been well into their nineties and possibly early hundreds. Both were extraordinary characters who continued to live in a bygone age that is now all but forgotten.

Daisy and Edith lived a life of supreme opulence, and cared little for modern life. When they couldn't attend church, the church attended them, at home. When they needed the attention of their bank manager or solicitor, both financial and legal advice moved from the office to their wonderful home.

This arrived together with *The Daily Telegraph*, morning milk, groceries, fresh fish and newly baked bread. It seemed that the entire world was at the beck and call of the Misses Bentley. They tended to take tea with whoever needed to call, always by appointment and always on time, at the precise hour of four in the afternoon.

These two fine ladies arose daily with the sun, despite the fact that they had absolutely nothing else to do all day. A summer's morning would find them in their immaculate kitchen at 5am, preparing for the day ahead. This would involve baking and tidying an already pristine kitchen and making sure that the house was in a condition to receive visitors later in the day, of which there were many. In spring and summer they would venture early into the garden to tend their precious blooms, where they would don straw hats and move around their exquisite garden, clippers in hand and trug over the arm.

By 8am they had done most of the work, despite the fact that Fanny, "the lady what obliges", was yet to arrive to clean the house from top to bottom. Rivers, the gardener, would follow Fanny; and at fifteen minutes to four on two afternoons a week, I would arrive, to sit with these wonderful people. The reason for my visits was simply to make sure they were all right and to offer them a degree of comfort. The reason for me arriving at the precise time of 3.45pm was that I knew they would always say: "Oh Chris! How delighted we are to see you! You must stay for tea whilst you are here."

Tea in the Bentley household was an institution in itself. There would usually be a guest, whether it be the vicar, the bank manager, solicitor, local councillor or simply a very entertaining and unusual person, the likes of whom Daisy and Ethel knew in droves. At their fine table I have met people from all walks of life and heard tales that would fill volumes with fascinating writings. The company seemed to be secondary to the ritual of the tea itself. Bone china of the finest quality was always used, the almost transparent porcelain cups filled from a solid-silver tea service and the tea brewed from leaves that came from packets bearing the names of either Fortnum & Mason, Harrods or Taylors of Harrogate. Teabags were unknown; whist tea strainers and slop bowls were de rigueur. If China tea was to be served, thin slices of freshly cut lemon were available and milk was absent. Otherwise, the teas varied in flavour but were always served with the same charming ritual.

The tea table was always laden with freshly baked cakes, scones and bread. Cream appeared in endless abundance, and jams, preserves and meat pastes were always homemade and tasty in the extreme. In summer, raspberries and strawberries would find their way from the garden to the table and be consumed with relish, reminding one of the tastes of one's youth.

Such was the timeless gentility of this household that it seemed nothing could possibly go wrong. These ladies were perfection personified and managed their entire day to a closely observed timetable. Over breakfast, the newspaper would be delivered and read, the crossword completed and the mail opened and dealt with. A change of clothes would be necessary for morning coffee, where the agenda for the rest of the day would be discussed. Lunch would either be taken at the local hostelry or prepared and eaten at home in the conservatory. The early afternoon would involve a game of Scrabble or Lexicon, followed by afternoon tea and then a little siesta. Tea was the last big meal of the day, supper consisting merely of a bowl of homemade soup and fresh bread taken whilst playing a game of cards, usually canasta. Television, whilst available, was simply accessed for the news or the occasional documentary.

Whilst they loved one another dearly, they would be prone to argue from time to time, and this would usually involve a difference of opinion on the state of the world, or a difficult clue in *The Daily Telegraph* crossword. Sometimes the argument was so serious that one could sense an atmosphere that could be cut with a knife. One afternoon, I sensed just such an atmosphere but, before I relate it, I feel that I must recall three other incidents that epitomise the character of these fine ladies and show the wicked sense of fun that was hidden under the clipped exterior of their daily lives.

The first occurred one spring afternoon, when both sisters were in unusually high spirits. I guessed that the stock market must have done rather well that morning, as it was clear that both had partaken of an ample portion of their favourite tipple, Harvey's Bristol Cream sherry, over lunch. Daisy was particularly vocal as she asked whether I would like sugar in my tea. As I declined, I noticed that she already had a huge sugar lump poised over my cup. My refusal, coupled with her obvious inebriation, caused the tongs to part and the huge sugar lump to fall teawards with an enormous PLOP that caused many droplets of dark brown tea to splash all over the newly starched tablecloth.

"Oh bums!" exclaimed Daisy.

The silence that ensued was palpable, broken only by a feeble voice issuing from Daisy herself, trying to cover for her unheard-of use of a supposed swear word by repeating time after time: 'Oh crumbs, Oh tums.'

Another incident involved Edith and happened shortly after tea, when it had been decided to play a rather raucous game called 'Bargain', which involved bidding for a card by trying to shout out the name of the commodity needed to complete a series, above the shouts of your opponents. The more the tea guests – that included the vicar – shouted, the more excited Edith became. I suppose it was inevitable that Edith would slip from her chair onto the floor, landing with an unceremonious crash as she shouted her bid of "Corn, Corn, Corn!" in response to my equally loud "Sugar, Sugar, Sugar!" What was totally unexpected was the extreme rush of air from her backside as she broke uncontrollable wind whilst falling to the floor.

Poor Edith spent the rest of the afternoon moving furniture backwards and forwards across the room in the faint hope of replicating the sound of the offending fart that had caused such hilarity, and such embarrassment to her, in order that she might shift the blame onto something else.

The third incident was mild in comparison. I arrived a little late and found the vicar already partaking of tea. I took my place at the table, but not before I noticed that the Scrabble board had been in use and had been covered by a strategically placed tea towel. I removed the towel to find the word SEX very prominently in the middle of the board.

Realising that the tea towel had been hastily placed there on the arrival of the vicar, so as to spare him from the sight of such a strong word over tea, I duly replaced it without mention. The vicar, however, was not so reticent and reached over me with glee, exclaiming, "I love Scrabble!" as he whipped off the tea towel, revealing the offending word. A difficult silence ensued, that I have since found to be almost unique.

Lastly, and this involves the atmosphere that I spoke of earlier, I came across a situation that once again involved a game of Scrabble and left me with the distinct impression that nothing is ever as it first seems. I had arrived at my allotted time of 3.45pm and found Daisy extremely distraught. To say that she was beside herself would be an understatement.

"Whatever is the matter?" I asked.

"I am most terribly upset," came the reply. "Edith has just cheated at Scrabble. We have an unwritten agreement that nobody cheats and that we must all follow the *Oxford Dictionary*. Edith has cheated and claims that she has won the game."

"How has she cheated?' I asked, knowing how they valued each other's knowledge of the English language.

"She has used a swear word," said Daisy, almost in tears at the enormity of the situation.

"Whatever word has she used to make you so upset?" I tried to reassure her, feeling the enormity of the word was about to be disclosed.

"She has used the word URINAL, despite the fact that we have always agreed that we will never, ever use swear words."

"But urinal is not a swear word, and it is in the dictionary as a proper word," I replied, trying to make light of a serious situation.

"I will have you know, young man," she continued, "that the word URINAL involves the toiletry habits and functions of men and that it must therefore be deemed to be a swear word of the worst kind. I will also inform you that had I been so inclined I could have gone out before Edith if I had cheated as she has now. I could have used an equally wrong word. I could have gone out with the word BUGGER."

Wondering what to do next, I made for the drawing room, where an extraordinary sight met me. The local publican and Edith were literally rolling about with laughter on the sofa, and the vicar was sitting bolt upright on his chair with a look on his face that suggested he had been let into a secret of some dreadful scandal. The Scrabble board and letters lay strewn over the floor as if swept aside in a fit of violent temper. This was going to take some sorting out and would test my diplomacy as a care worker to the absolute limit.

Going back through my diaries, I was reminded of an occurrence last spring that involved a rather cute reptile, or *Testudinidae* to give it its scientific name, that I feel is worth relating, as it shows how one can be compromised by the strange requests of our clients, and shows the ability of people to overcome their disabilities.

4th March 2006

Timmy Tortoise

Today has served to remind me of the great capacity of the human brain to overcome difficulties, and the fact that whenever one of our senses begins to deteriorate another tends to strengthen in compensation. This was graphically demonstrated to me this morning when I paid my first visit to Alan Fuller, a retired local dentist, much loved in the community, who lived on his own in a large bungalow on the outskirts of town.

His wife had sadly passed away some years ago, but he insisted on living on his own despite the fact that he had almost completely lost his sight. He also suffered from other physical disabilities that caused some pain and major difficulties with his mobility, which was the reason why our organisation visited him every morning to help him get up and to prepare his breakfast.

Being my first visit I had to find my way around his home, but was greatly assisted by Alan, who seemed to be able to sense or hear exactly where I was in the house.

"I can't find any socks!" I shouted from across his vast bedroom.

"Try the second drawer down on the other chest of drawers; I never keep them in that drawer," he replied, although I was convinced that he couldn't actually see where I was.

I tried the drawer he described and, sure enough, loads of socks! The next task was to 'find incontinence pads', which I had been told were in the cupboard, so I began to search the many bedroom cupboards, which proved fruitless and led to an ever widening hunt that involved cupboards in the hall, bathrooms and other bedrooms. Just as I was about to open another door he shouted:

"Not that one!"

Too late, I thought, as the door, which was suffering from a distinct lack of hinges, fell inwards and landed with an almighty crash on the floor.

"We never use that one, as we haven't fixed the hinges yet, so the door's just propped up in the frame. [I could have told him that!] Try the next room."

The next room proved fruitful and I was much relieved to find it stacked almost to the ceiling with boxes of medical paraphernalia, some of which contained incontinence pads. I selected a box and returned to the bedroom to continue my tasks, with everything going according to the instructions, until I finally got Alan comfortably settled in his favourite chair. I had made toast, brewed a cup of tea, prompted medication, placed a cold drink beside him, secured his slippers onto his feet and switched on the radio. He then made a very strange request:

"Would you be an awfully good fellow and look out into the garden for me, to check on Timothy?"

"I thought you lived alone; who is Timothy?" I replied, a little confused, as I hadn't seen any evidence of anyone else around the house. I opened the curtains and could see no one.

"There's no one there, I'm afraid," I said, somewhat confused.

"You'll have to actually go out and find Timothy. I expect the grass has got a little long and you can't see him from the window, unless of course he has gone back into hibernation. Poor old Timmy Tortoise is over forty years old, you know, so he may be a little sleepy, although the weather has been unseasonably warm for early spring."

Ah! So, Timmy was a tortoise. No wonder I couldn't see him from the window. I opened the French doors and searched the lawn and the borders. No sign of him. Perhaps I should search the rockery, as there appeared to be some rather tortoise-shaped rocks around that area. I found Timmy near the pond, snuggled in to his large tortoise shell, and returned to the lounge to report my success.

"I found him on the rockery, but he seems to be asleep," I reported, pleased that I was able to be of some service.

"Then, please would you go back and tell him that Dad is okay and that Granddaughter will be along next week to make him comfy in his bed for the summer."

I returned to the rockery, a little nervous to be speaking to a tortoise whilst there might be prying eyes watching from neighbours' windows. Feeling sure that Timmy wouldn't be able to understand me, I whispered to him that his dad was okay, and not to concern himself with coming out of hibernation. I was also aware that it would appear to any bystanders that I was actually talking to a rock!

"I may be blinking blind, but I am not bloody deaf!" Alan shouted. "Now, tell Timmy what I asked, so that I can hear you. After all, he is over forty years old and he may be getting a little deaf himself, not to mention the fact that his little head is inside a shell."

I glanced up at the windows next door and felt sure I saw curtains fluttering. Anyone seeing me would think that I was talking to the fish in the pond or to the lone stone gnome who was dangling his fishing rod into the water. Covered in acute embarrassment and turning the colour of overripe strawberries, I decided to take the bull by the horns and shout as requested. I leant over within a couple of feet of Timmy.

"I've just popped along to tell you that Dad is okay!" I screamed at the top of my voice. "And Granddaughter is coming to acclimatise you to the summer next week!"

The next-door curtains were working overtime, but I felt strangely satisfied that I had in some way helped and encouraged an elderly tortoise and been able to set his mind at rest before his total emergence into the spring and summer sun. I did, however, wonder whether there would be two men in white coats outside the front door, waiting to take me away for treatment for some mental illness.

Returning to the lounge, I was warmly thanked by Alan, who assured me that I would always be welcome in his house, as long as I got on with Timothy.

This reminded me that you should never assume that because someone is blind, they are blind in spirit as well as sight – and also that their hearing can be more acute than most people's. Never try to get one over on a person with a sensory disability, or you will get found out.

With these thoughts going through my mind, I pondered on the fact that those with physical disabilities were very similar in their outlook, in that they usually found ways to compensate for their physical problems and overcome them. I had met one such man last Christmas, who had gone to extreme lengths to conquer his difficulties.

14th December 2005
The inventor

December is always considered a very special month among those working in the care sector. We are acutely aware that many of our service users find themselves alone and isolated over Christmas, and we do our best to make sure they have a chance of some of the enjoyment that we tend to take for granted. I love working on Christmas Day so I can make sure that my more vulnerable clients have a visit from me, usually around lunchtime, when I pull a cracker with them as they tuck into their Christmas lunch which has been so expertly provided by the local 'meals on wheels' service. My daughter always asks me why I don't bring them all home for the day and I have to reply that I simply don't have the facilities to cope with about twenty people who have varying degrees of disability. Whilst assessing my commitments over the Christmas period, it is always heartening to find a client who needs no help and is supported by a family which lives close by.

Today is just such a day and, as I arrive at the Pillsbury family home, I am confident that Leonard will experience no loneliness over the festive period. Len, my notes tell me, is suffering from a rare form of Parkinson's disease. He doesn't display the usual symptoms of trembling limbs and communication problems, but does have a severe balance difficulty that causes him to fall over with predictable regularity.

It was obvious, on viewing the situation as I pulled into the drive, that the Pillsbury bungalow was undergoing significant extensions and alterations, evident from the mounds of building materials that almost blocked my progress to the front door. Having navigated the obstacle course that apologised for a path, I pressed the bell and unleashed a sequence that tickled my sense of humour. Firstly the chimes of Big Ben sounded, followed by a recorded message, which starkly stated:

"You have reached the gatekeeper of the Pillsbury residence. Should you wish to move forward from this point it must be stressed that we accept no visits from complete strangers, hawkers, tinkers, double-glazing salesmen, persons involved in any way with utility companies or anyone who has no business to be standing on this doorstep. Should you wish to continue this call, please press the bell again."

I duly pressed the button.

"You have now entered the second stage of entry to this humble abode. Please lift the flap below the bell push and remove the phone. Only do this if you have the best of intentions, as any attempt to deceive will be met by a small electric shock to the ear and hand. You have been warned!"

I lifted the flap, removed the phone from its cradle, put it to my ear and waited for a response.

"Do you have an appointment?"

"Yes," I replied. "I have come from the care agency to sit with Mr Pillsbury whilst Mrs Pillsbury goes Christmas shopping."

"Please follow the instructions that are about to be given."

I was grateful for the lack of an electric shock, as I realised that I was still talking to a machine, and was much relieved when the door opened, revealing a human being in the elegant form of Mrs Janine Pillsbury.

"Please excuse the rather 'Heath Robinson' attempt at a door entry system, but Len gets carried away with his inventions and rather puts people off calling. The trouble is that whenever anyone has almost managed to negotiate the entry system, they get bored and tend to wander away, so I do try to intervene, but Len insists that I use his system to its full potential, to eliminate unnecessary callers. However, you are most welcome. Please come in and meet the genius."

Janine was one of those ladies of advanced years who had retained a beauty that could have graced the pages of the most expensive upper-class fashion magazines. I followed her into a lounge filled with musical instruments, from a grand piano to a harpsichord and various guitars. Wind, brass and stringed instruments were spread about with apparent abandonment. I was intrigued.

"Excuse the mess," she exclaimed. "We are both musicians and our instruments tend to stay where we last played them. I play various keyboards, and Len tries to play stringed pieces. We were both in an orchestra, but poor old Len finds it difficult now, due to his disability, so he tends to get more involved with his inventions these days."

As she spoke, I became aware of a distant sound that could only be described as a commotion. The sound grew closer and louder, like some traction engine that was malfunctioning, an intermittent puffing and crashing, getting ever nearer to the door of the lounge. Suddenly an apparition appeared, in the form of Len, dressed from top to toe in protective skateboarder's attire, a purple helmet adorning his splendid head. He rounded the doorway on one wheel of his Zimmer frame, made towards me and promptly fell at my feet.

"Hello, I'm Len, SUPERHERO, known locally as ZIMMERMAN!"

He got himself up, dusted himself down and continued:

"So sorry to have fallen – which must be the hundredth fall today! But never mind, as we're here to discuss the plight of people like me who tend to fall for no apparent reason and to find ways to improve our lot. I am an inventor who has invented loads of devices to improve the lives of people just like me."

I was immediately intrigued by this man and asked what he had invented.

"Well," he replied, "I have invented a drinking device for people who have the trembles and wobbles. You will have noticed that anyone who has uncontrolled shakes will spill most of their drink over themselves and the carpet. I have experimented with a device that tilts with the head, to dispense liquid into the mouth whenever the head is bent forward.

"However, the forward movement of the head, together with the backward movement of the receptacle, meant that the liquid met the mouth before the mouth had reached the desired angle. This resulted in liquid being inhaled into the nose rather than the mouth, which invariably caused a situation of extreme choking.

"To resolve this situation I devised a pumping and pneumatic apparatus, which meant that when the chin was lowered, it operated a pump which in turn drew liquid from the bottle into the mouth cavity, which, when swallowed, delivered an amount of life-sustaining fluid into the digestive system without the problem of the trembles. Simple, really, but very effective."

I was impressed.

"Have you invented anything else?" I enquired.

By this time his wife had left, and I was to spend the next two hours being entertained by this incredible man.

"Oh yes, indeed," he replied. "I have invented the means of holding a musical instrument without the need for the support of hands. Whether it is a violin, viola, oboe or flute, my device, which works on support from the sternum, or breastbone, eliminates the need for anyone with a disability to actually hold an instrument. They only have to blow, pluck or bow with one hand, whilst stopping frets or holes with the other, to produce beautiful sounds, without the need to physically hold the instrument."

He gave me an impromptu demonstration with the violin, leaving me wondering whether such an invention was ready to be launched on a hitherto unsuspecting public.

"But I have also invented something really special that will help all sufferers of diseases that cause people to fall over with loss of balance. Please come to my workshop and I will demonstrate it to you."

I followed him to his workshop and watched as he threaded a length of wire from his slippers, inside the legs of his trousers, through the inside of his shirt and round his neck to a terminal on his helmet. He attached one end of the wire to a metallic device under his toes and the other to a lamp, which was appended to a long piece of metal rod that extended from his helmet.

"This is a device to warn me that I am about to fall over," he stated with supreme confidence, "and I am about to show you how it works."

He made his way to the hall, limping all the while from the equipment that impeded his left foot, and proceeded to set off at a goodly pace down the hall. I watched with my mouth slightly open and my eyes agog at the enormity of the situation that was about to be unleashed. About halfway down the hall he came to a crashing halt as he fell, arms, legs and wires flailing in the air.

"That didn't work very well," I said, trying not to be hurtful.

"On the contrary, my dear friend. I may have fallen, but at least I knew that it was about to happen. Maybe the device needs a modicum of tweaking here and there!"

Len is such an impressive character. He hasn't let his disability affect his life or his sense of fun. On the contrary, he has used his considerable talents in the pursuit of helping others.

28th November 2006

Burnt toast

The ability to overcome extreme disability and limited life expectancy and to be cheerful and upbeat about one's problems always inspires me. One of the strongest characters I ever met was Kevin, who had a very serious and progressive condition that after a short time would lead to the inevitable outcome. Kevin had Parkinson's disease, which was not an unusual affliction to me, though it affected people in many different ways. I had experience of a large number of people with this debilitating and incurable illness that ravaged the body as it crept onwards to inevitable death. The path toward this inevitability was always hard to witness for the carer, and one hundred times more difficult for the families of those concerned. What starts as a mild illness develops gradually and cruelly. It takes away firstly the mobility, then the ability to communicate and finally the ability to swallow or breath effectively.

The really hard part of this particular illness is that the mental capacity remains intact, so that while there is great and increasing suffering, the brain knows exactly what is going on but the body is unable to respond or, in the latter stages, communicate. What amazed me and inspired me was the ability of many sufferers to accept their fate and remain cheerful. Kevin, who I am visiting today, is just such a man.

He had a passion for all sports, but particularly cricket, which he had played avidly for years, until struck down with this awful disease. His sons were equally sporty and would spend many hours with their dad watching test cricket.

He had a loving and loyal family, something which no doubt kept his spirits up. His devoted wife June lovingly cared for him day in and day out until she too became unwell and had to call in social services to find some help, to give her some respite. Somehow she also managed to hold down a very responsible job, to try to maintain the family finances.

By the time I arrived on the scene, Kevin was just about able to transfer from a chair or bed into a wheelchair, and I would often take him out for a drive, or to do a little shopping. It gave June respite, and Kevin really enjoyed our little trips. He could still eat normally and would always seek out a tube of Rolos, which he would share with me.

Unhappily, these trips didn't last long, as his condition deteriorated and it was no longer safe to transfer him into and out of the car. By this time he was now transferring by hoist within the house, having all his drinks thickened and solid food liquidised. But still he did everything with a smile.

I remember the time I arrived at his house to find smoke billowing out of the front door, smoke alarm sounding and a very strong smell of thoroughly burnt toast. Forgetting all advice on dealing with emergency fire situations, I threw open the front door, knowing that the kitchen lay just to the right of the entrance. I also knew that if a fire had occurred near the grill, Kevin had no chance of getting past it in his wheelchair.

As I entered the kitchen it became apparent that Kevin was not in there. The room was filled with smoke, and the floor was littered with slices of cremated toast. The grill was still on full power, although the grill pan was now empty but very, very hot. However, there was no evidence of the possibility of fire.

I turned off the grill, opened the windows and armed myself with a newspaper to flap against the smoke detector to try to silence it, and went in search of Kevin.

I entered the lounge, and in the corner by the window was Kevin, grinning from ear to ear but looking a little sheepish, like a naughty schoolboy. His smile meant that I couldn't be cross, although he had broken a number of house rules that applied when he was on his own. One of those rules forbade him to eat or drink, as he was very susceptible to choking, and he couldn't possibly eat toast, as this could potentially be fatal. It transpired that he had undergone an irresistible urge to eat toast, and had been careful in his preparation, though hadn't anticipated dozing off in his wheelchair, to be awoken by the smoke alarm. In panic, he had pulled the flaming bread from the grill and fled, or wheeled his way, to the supposed safety of the lounge. I pointed out to him that, should a fire have developed, he would have most certainly been trapped.

I had to inform the office of the incident, and it was some time before I got Kevin's confidence back, as he was very cross that June had been informed of his silly mistake.

As his condition deteriorated I spent more time with him, feeding him and persuading him to drink thickened cups of tea and coffee that looked, quite frankly, awful. I had to be there while he attempted to drink, in case he choked. By this time, June had undergone an operation and couldn't do anything that involved lifting, so she needed more and more help.

One day, while June was shopping, Kevin decided he wanted to watch the test match. He had great difficulty operating the remote control, as his brain told him what to do but his body operated with several seconds' delay between the brain signal and the bodily action.

This meant that we were often left with a blank screen and no idea how to restore it. When it comes to technology I am completely at a loss, so I was not of any help in such situations. If I press the wrong button on my own remote control I often have to phone my son for advice.

However, this day the test match seemed to be in full swing, when suddenly it went off and we were faced with a blank screen. Kevin pressed button after button, and the television set seemed to be deranged, changing from channel to channel with gay abandon, which was completely appropriate, as it seemed to get stuck on some distant gay sex channel!

I gave up and Kevin gave up, but the look on June's face when she entered the room to find two grown men watching a gay sex channel on the television was a picture. June had a wicked sense of humour and I never lived that day down.

Kevin continued in his decline but remained ever cheerful, even when he had to have a 'PEG feed' installed. He continued to try to do whatever he could for himself, including washing, teeth cleaning, etc. He was determined to enjoy his last days, knowing that the end would come soon. He was younger than me by quite a few years, but by this time seemed a lot older.

One day, whilst chasing trespassers out of our garden, I slipped on some wet leaves on the hillside and fell rather awkwardly on my left foot. I glanced down and noticed that my foot was at a rather odd angle with respect to my ankle. I pulled it back into shape, enduring considerable pain, assuming I had dislocated my ankle, and staggered back to the house. I was on duty at the time and phoned the 'on-call' to explain what had happened and to say that I would continue the calls unless the pain and swelling got worse. I then got into the car and drove to Bournemouth to visit a client, followed by a trip to see Kevin. The pain was extreme, especially when I applied the clutch.

On arriving at Kevin's house I rang the doorbell, walking stick in hand, dreading climbing the front doorstep. June answered the door and said:

"What on earth is wrong with you?"

"I've just sprained my ankle. There's nothing to worry about," I replied, holding back my expression of extreme pain.

"Get you to hospital NOW!" was her response.

So I drove home, to be met by my son, who took me to hospital where, following X-rays, it was found that I had not only broken my ankle in two places but had fractured my leg in two places also.

This meant an operation to put metal plates in my ankle and leg, and twelve weeks off work. I was to be reminded of this accident for years afterwards as I often set off alarms at airport security.

Sadly it also meant that I never saw Kevin again, as he died in hospital a few days later. I was unable to attend his funeral, as my ability to walk was severely impaired. I was told at the time that you know when you are about to get better once you have mastered the art of walking on crutches. How true that is. I had a terrible problem with the walking aids initially, and it wasn't until just before I was to have the plaster removed that I became adept in the use of crutches.

It was sad that I never saw Kevin again, but he did leave behind a remarkable memory – that nothing was as bad as it seemed and that there were always people worse off than yourself. He was a courageous and lovely man who will be fondly remembered by all who came into contact with him.

Kevin, rest in peace without the pain and suffering of your illness. May your legacy simply be that you taught all who came into contact with you that the frailty and shortness of human life, where any future is unpredictable, and the inevitability of death, no matter what our age, is something that we must face, with courage and confidence, and never sadness.

You left a legacy that will remain for generations – that of dealing with the undealable, coping with the inevitable, and all the while putting a shine to other people's lives by remaining forever optimistic and cheerful in life.

4th December 2006
The lost toes

Care work often entails keeping a watchful eye on a client for various reasons, and I have got quite used to looking for symptoms that may herald the need for assistance. However, I am totally unprepared for the instructions that I have been given this morning. My line manager has phoned and asked me to visit a new client who has just been discharged from hospital. He was admitted some two weeks previously with the possible onset of gangrene to his toes. He had received such treatment that prevented the awful likelihood of amputation of his right foot. However, they were unable to save the life of two of his toes, which were still attached to his foot but were unlikely to stay there much longer. My instructions were unusual, and stomach churning.

"Mr Eric Legg requires a full strip wash and shave, assistance to dress and the liberal application of aqueous cream to his entire body. Particular care must be taken with the toes of his right foot and the office informed immediately if his two diseased toes become detached from his foot!"

To say that I was a little uneasy would be understating my feelings as I began to take in the enormity of the instructions that I had just been given. What they had singularly failed to tell me was what I was supposed to do with the said toes if they became detached. Should I put them in a plastic sandwich bag and put them in the fridge or freezer? Leave them on the floor and call for help? Put them out with the rubbish (either general, recycling or compost)? Pop them in a bag and take them to the office? Or just panic and run?! However, being quite used to unusual requests, I made my way to the client's address and introduced myself.

It was clear that his left foot was heavily bandaged and that it would be foolish for me to try to wash it. I was relieved and particularly pleased to hear that the district nurse was calling every day to attend to his medical needs. I was pleased to perform all the other tasks and was grateful to be able to put a sock over the bandage.

After my morning round, I called the office to check that I had heard the instructions correctly. Charlotte signified in the affirmative and apologised for giving me such an unusual and seemingly gruesome task. She also apologised for cutting off the phone conversation but remarked that the very thought of the task had made her feel a little queasy and she had felt unable to finish the instructions. She continued that were I to find the toes detached, I was to phone the office, who would call the doctor to visit the client and make sure all was well. It would be advisable to place the toes in a suitable receptacle that should then be covered with a plastic bag. They would need to be examined!

1st March 2007
And so to bed

Gerald Merryweather was a true gentleman and it was always a pleasure to visit him. I went to see him on the third Wednesday of every month whilst his wife went out with her sister. Gerald had very complex needs and many health problems, including arthritis, asthma, digestive disorders and a dodgy heart, but perhaps his most interesting problems were his narcolepsy and his epilepsy.

Before my first visit to people who have illnesses or disabilities that I have not experienced before, I always do a little research into the disorders by looking in my Caxton's *Family Physician* manual, which lists most ailments. The fact that this trusty encyclopaedia was first printed in 1930 and last reprinted in 1954 probably accounts for the omission of some of the health complaints that I encounter. For example, it would appear that narcolepsy didn't exist in 1954, and the description of epilepsy is somewhat alarming. It reads:

During the course of normal daily activity there comes a moment when the brain fails! The preliminary symptoms may take the form of memories of places, of a bar of music, of a sensation of smell of jam making or of a flower: sometimes voices are heard and sometimes the ringing of bells. Almost immediately afterwards the patient gives a short cry, throws out his arms and falls down with a thud. He or She becomes immediately unconscious. The face goes into spasms, becoming purple and even black, the eyes twitch, the breathing becomes stertorous, there is frothing at the mouth and the convulsions take place in the arms and legs. It must be remembered that in the period immediately following the fit, the person has no mental resistance and may even become homicidal. It is wrong to treat epileptics as criminals because of misdeeds resulting from the disease.

Alarming stuff indeed, and the bit about homicidal tendencies made me a little nervous! Perhaps in this instance it would be best to have the illness explained by his wife and ignore the advice of years gone by. However, I knew that I would feel very wary if I caught the aroma of jam-making as I walked through the door.

When I arrived at Jean and Gerald Merryweather's home, I was struck by the peace and serenity of it. Jean made me feel most welcome and explained Gerald's problems before I went into the lounge to meet him. Gerald had been a master thatcher until he was thirty-five years old, when he had suddenly developed epilepsy. The fact that he spent most of his working days on roofs and ladders meant that it would have been unwise to continue in that occupation, so he had effectively retired at a very early age.

Latterly, apart from his previously stated health problems, he had developed narcolepsy. It was interesting to learn that this illness meant that he was liable to fall asleep on frequent occasions, so care had to be taken when drinking hot fluids, as he might fall asleep and scald himself. She explained that he liked a cup of steaming hot Bovril and two Jammy Dodgers before he went to bed. I was to have whatever I liked from the larder.

He would want to go to bed as soon as he got seriously tired, which was difficult to assess due to his narcolepsy.

Until bedtime he would want to watch television, but due to his hearing difficulties would be unable to hear it unless it was turned up to full volume. Don't let him do this, or you will also end up with hearing difficulties, but put on the subtitles instead. If he suffers a fit, leave him alone and dial 999. It is unlikely that he will have one as he only had one last night.

With the instructions fresh in my mind, I was taken into the lounge to meet Gerald. He was asleep, so I wished Jean a very good evening and sat down beside him to keep him company for the next four hours. *Coronation Street* was on the television, so I changed channels to get the evening news on BBC 2.

He immediately woke up and was somewhat surprised to see a total stranger sitting next to him, and I guess I would have been a little concerned had I been in the same situation. I quickly explained to him who I was and why I was sitting in his lounge, watching his television and looking at his evening paper. He failed to understand, and I quickly realised that this could be due to his deafness. Not wanting to induce a fit through unnecessary stress, I wrote my name and the reason for my visit on a piece of paper and showed it to him. He visibly relaxed and held out his hand in welcome, which I took as he fell back into another deep sleep. When he awoke we went through the introductions again and settled into a very pleasant period of conversation.

It soon became apparent that his hearing was not as bad as I had been led to believe, particularly after he had inserted a hearing aid into each ear. He also had the ability to lip-read once he had got used to my speech. Gerald was of very short stature and had a face that made one feel at instant peace with the world. It was kindly and understanding, and he clearly loved life, despite his severe disabilities. He talked quite openly about his problems and gave me an idea of the signs to look for when he had an approaching fit.

"My left knee will start jerking and my leg will begin to shake. I may throw my head backwards, and then I will enter into a major fit. At this point, just leave me alone and dial 999. It will probably be necessary for me to be taken to hospital until I am stabilised."

From that moment I noticed that his left knee had a permanent twitch and that both of his legs shook continuously. However, he fell asleep again and remained asleep for the next two hours, at which point I noticed that the twitching seemed to be getting worse. I woke him up and asked if he would like his Bovril, to which he replied in the affirmative. We sat for the next hour drinking our drinks and exchanging rather doubtful and risqué jokes. He was extremely good company during that hour and I was sorry when he said that he wanted to go to bed.

The process of getting him from the chair, into the bathroom, onto the toilet and thence into the bedroom took up the entire remaining hour, as he tended to drop off to sleep whenever he paused or sat down. It was a battle to keep him awake, but once in bed he became totally alert and expressed a desire to get back up again and watch a little more television. I felt a little apprehensive; I was worried that Jean would be surprised if she found him up and wide awake when she returned. I needn't have worried as, by the time I had fetched his stick, he had dropped off into another phase of narcolepsy and was snoring loudly. I pulled the covers up to his neck, turned out the light and returned to the lounge to watch television. When Jean finally arrived back home I too was asleep and all was peaceful.

I continued to visit Gerald for the next two years, and we became firm friends. He never suffered a fit whilst under my care, but I remained vigilant for that twitch of the knee that might signal one. Gerald taught me a lot about life, as he appeared to have a natural insight into many of the world's problems. I suppose the years he had spent in contemplation whilst sitting in his favourite chair, watching television and reading countless books, had educated him well beyond his school years.

Dear old Gerald died last year, aged ninety-four, and I miss his wise and sometimes humorous conversation. He had a rotten life health-wise but didn't let it impede his infectious happiness.

2nd April 2007
Party time

Today has something different in store. Peter Wells' son is marrying his childhood sweetheart at the parish church of St James in the centre of Poole, followed by a lavish reception at The Mansion House hotel. I am to accompany him, as he needs constant supervision owing to his condition. My presence will give his wife, Mary, the chance to enjoy the proceedings and mix with friends and relatives, giving a little respite to her constant vigilance. I am purely there in a work capacity but will still enjoy the day, which will give me a chance to see a happier side to the Wells family, although Peter never complains and remains ever cheerful.

The service went really well and I noticed some hankies being used to wipe away tears of joy. At the conclusion of the service, confetti was thrown, despite the plea from the vicar not to use it. A gleaming silver vintage Rolls Royce pulled up to transport the happy couple to the reception, which was only a hundred yards away. The driver took them for a round trip of the town before dropping them off, so that they could get value for money for the hire of such an expensive car. Tourists along Poole Quay cheered as they passed and added to the splendid occasion.

At the reception, champagne was flowing before the lavish buffet was served. I had to be careful to stay on soft drinks, due to the regulations on alcohol within the care organisation, and also keep a close eye on Pete, who needed to drink through a straw. He had to settle for plain wine as the bubbles might have affected him.

The time for the service of the buffet arrived with a strident announcement from a red-coated toastmaster. It took me back to my catering days, years before, when I had served many lavish buffets. He also said that there was plenty for all and not to all rush up at once. As usual the opposite happened, and everyone, apart from the bridal party, jumped up and hurried to join the scrum that was forming around the buffet, with people piling their plates high with delicious food. I hoped there would be enough food to last until I got up to get a plateful for Peter after the greedy rush had subsided.

I thought back to the days of my catering career and one particular function stood out in my mind. It was a very embarrassing moment in my life but I still chuckle at the memory. I had been requested to supply and serve a buffet for the trustees of the RNLI, which was to be served on an island in the middle of Poole Harbour. The island was owned by a local millionaire and had five houses dotted around and a quaint chalet with a large patio that looked out on the distant town of Poole.

It was a haven of peace, as the only full-time residents were the island's caretaker/boatman and his wife.

The guest list was impressive, the chairman being none other than the Duke of Atholl, the owner of a vast estate of over 130,000 acres and a private army. I believe that he is the only duke to have his own army, a privilege granted by some distant monarch. There was also another duke, though I've forgotten where his dukedom was. There were a number of other very important people, including Raymond Baxter, the television presenter of *Tomorrow's World*. I was determined to impress, as the RNLI has its headquarters in Poole and this function could generate extra business.

All was ready, and the buffet table sagged with half lobsters, dressed crabs, decorated salmons and various meats, including a whole cooked ham on which I had decorated the flag of the RNLI. This was to be an elegant buffet and not one that would follow the usual mad rush to cram food onto the plate; I would have liked the Duke of Atholl to be first so that I could show off my handiwork, then the ladies could help themselves, followed by the gentlemen.

Imagine my surprise when I espied a rather untidy looking gentleman, with patches on the elbows of his blue sweater, at the buffet table, plate and cutlery in hand, about to select some fish. I assumed that he was the boatman, and moved forward to put a stop to this unacceptable behaviour. I asked him to leave the buffet until all the guests had been fed and then he could have what was left over. I took him to a back room and asked him to stay there. I was equally disturbed by the cheeky, knowing grin that he gave me as I left him, as if he were saying that he would soon be getting his own back on me.

The problem being temporarily resolved, I was surprised to find all the guests waiting in silence, plates in hand, awaiting instructions. The owner of the island eventually came up to me to enquire as to whether I had seen the Duke of Atholl, as it would be a good idea if he was the first to be served, as chair of the committee. I asked what he looked like and he replied:

"Well, he doesn't look anything like a duke. Quite the opposite, in fact. He looks more like a seasoned sailor, wearing a blue sweater with patches on the elbows. In fact, he is the only one dressed for the sea crossing to this island."

Filled with embarrassment I realised the enormity of what I had done and hurried to the back room, where I found the duke, this time almost crying with laughter. He had got his own back, but I was relieved that he didn't seem cross. I apologised profusely and returned to a room full of laughing people. I felt that my mistake had somehow broken the ice and made the evening a far happier time. The duke insisted that I stopped calling him 'Your Grace', which I must say I found a little difficult. I was really impressed that an evening that I thought would be a rather snooty affair turned out to be a very friendly time, with no class barriers and lots of mirth. However, I digress once more.

Peter's son's wedding celebrations turned out to be another very happy day. There was plenty of food left after the initial rush, and I was able to get an ample plateful for Peter. At the end, I said my goodbyes to the happy couple and wished them all the best for the future, and then I took a very tired but happy Peter back home for a well-earned rest.

25th December 2006
More partying

Writing about one party always brings up reminders of other memorable parties. One took place on Christmas Day back in 2006, when I had volunteered to help with Christmas celebrations at a residential home that specialised in helping people with severe disabilities. Other memories took place some years back, one concerning a massive children's party, and the other a picnic for 300 disabled children, organised by the Variety Club of Great Britain.

Today is Christmas Day and I have volunteered to help with the lunchtime festivities at a residential home specialising in physical disabilities, run by my employer care organisation. On arrival it appeared that the party was already in full swing. There were volunteers in abundance and all of the care staff at the home had agreed to give their time free for the day. It would appear that helpers outnumbered the residents, and I was deeply moved to see so many people prepared to give up their own Christmas for those less fortunate. I wandered into the kitchen and found many more volunteers preparing a massive Yuletide feast.

Numbers were swelled by the attendance of a local charity, Canine Carers, which was a regular to this home and provided a valuable service. Its well-trained dogs provided a special companionship to these folk with extreme disabilities. This was truly a very happy, organised chaos. I began to wonder if I was superfluous, but soon realised that, as most of the residents needed one-to-one care while feeding, it would be all hands on deck.

Lunchtime duly arrived and I was allocated to a wonderful lady, who had such a disability that her food had to be liquidised and she needed to be fed with a spoon. I knew this lady well, as I had looked after her previously. All went well, until I dropped a morsel of food on the floor.

We were then inundated with the caring dogs, which began to beg on their hind legs for more food to be dropped. As if this wasn't enough, the gentleman on my right was having trouble with his sprouts, which were a shade undercooked and took some effort to cut with a knife.

Suddenly, whilst trying to cut one in half, the sprout slipped from the knife and flew across the table with some considerable velocity, landing in the eye of the lady sitting opposite. She screamed in pain, which started the dogs barking and a flurry of activity from all around. Who would believe that one brussel sprout could cause so much disruption, but the eye injury was felt to be so serious that the paramedics were called, and they duly arrived, fixed the eye problem and then joined the party.

Among other parties that spring to mind is one that I held whilst Mayor of Wimborne Minster, back in the late seventies. It was traditional that the mayor held a small reception for the great and good of the town at some time during the mayoral year. This was a low-key affair, as the budget didn't cover anything lavish. The mayor had an annual allowance of just £900 and that didn't go very far.

As the year that I served as mayor was also the Year of the Child, I decided to spend my entire budget on a children's party, open to all children in the town of school age and under fifteen. I was surprised that nearly 800 qualified, as I hadn't realised that the gentlefolk of Wimborne had been so prolific in producing children. It was also the time when the country had opened its borders to the unfortunate Vietnamese boat people. A refugee camp had been opened at nearby Sopley, so I decided to invite the children from there to the party as well. With so many children I had to divide the party into two days, one for the younger ones and one for the older ones. The youngest had the services of a clown, and the eldest a disco.

I have to say that the response from the town was superb. Town and district councillors acted as waiters and also helpers. They even formed a choir and gave a glorious rendition of 'Old MacDonald Had a Farm', much to the joy of the children, who made a huge noise with their attempts to outdo each other on the animal noise front. The clown and disco provided their services free of charge, and the local traders donated much of the food. I often wonder whether anyone living today remembers attending as a child.

The other party I remember very vividly is one that I catered for on Round Island in the middle of Poole Harbour. This was to be a 'Pirates' Day Out' party, organised by the Variety Club of Great Britain and purely for disabled children, who would number over 300.

The owner of the island, Harry Palmer, approached me to ask whether I could provide a picnic for them and the many helpers who would attend. The only proviso was that there was to be no funding whatsoever. I agreed to do the task and soon realised the enormity of providing nearly 400 picnics with no money to buy ingredients or to pay staff.

My first challenge was staffing, which was soon overcome by the generous offer of our longstanding staff member, Jill. Not only did she offer to work for nothing, but she also volunteered the help of her husband, John, and her two sons, Matthew and

Mark. My two children, Sarah and Peter, also agreed to help, not only with the party itself but also with the compilation of the picnic. Their many school friends also offered to help.

The next problem was food, and where to put it once prepared. As far as picnic containers were concerned, I had an acquaintance who worked for Virgin Atlantic Airlines. He had contacted Richard Branson and it had been agreed that, if I travelled to Heathrow Airport, I would be given everything I needed in the way of picnic packaging, together with balloons and anything else that may make the party go with a swing. Thanks to a local van-hire business, Tremaine Motors, I was able to travel to Heathrow with my great friend Bill Webber and fill a transit van with goodies from Virgin Atlantic. There was no cost, as the van hire was free, together with the petrol.

The problem of food was solved by some of my wonderful suppliers and local businesses. Soft drinks were provided free from Hall & Woodhouse Brewery, meat was provided at no cost from Jack Barker, the local butcher, fruit from the local greengrocers, cheese from my local cheese supplier, salad items from a local smallholding, and rolls, bread, crisps and nuts from our local Tesco store.

The only problem I had was procuring butter, as my main supplier, who will remain nameless, refused to give me twenty packs of butter for the party. Needless to say, I approached many other suppliers, and the first to agree to free butter got the contract for my catering business.

Having got everything together, we all dressed as pirates and made our way to Round Island, where we enjoyed a thoroughly successful event, which was also attended by such notables as Ron Moody, Ernie Wise and Captain Birdseye. The children had a great time, with Harry Palmer and friends driving them at manic speeds around the island in their various means of tractor transport.

What a day that was. The one great benefit of such a party is that there is no washing up afterwards – the provision of a dustbin was all we needed – and there is the added satisfaction of knowing that, whilst we earned absolutely zero, we made 300 children very happy. Well done, Harry Palmer, the Variety Club and my very loyal staff.

6th December 2007
I've been robbed!

Today started unremarkably but turned out to be a day to remember. I had called on Marcus MacTavish, as I have done for the last two years for four days every week. I shared his care with Colin, another male support worker, who had started work with us a short while ago and who I greatly admired for his caring and patient manner.

I had been able to assist with his induction and had imparted what little knowledge I had. This had been particularly useful in the case of Marcus, a lovely man who suffered from mild dementia yet still managed to stay at home alone.

Marcus had the unfortunate situation of having a back and a front door along the same side of his house, both with identical door chimes. This often led to hilarious consequences, as he rarely got to the right door first time round, but would open the wrong door, find no one there, close the door and make his way to the other one, which the caller had vacated to go to the other door they had heard open! This ritual would be repeated several times until the caller managed to arrive at an opening door at precisely the right time.

Marcus would jump at the sight of someone on the doorstep if he happened to open the right door first. It all depended on which part of the house he happened to be in at the moment of hearing the door chime. I got wise to this problem and rang the front door and stayed where I was in the certain knowledge that he would appear at some point. As long as there was a ringing doorbell, Marcus would continue to open doors until he found the cause.

Today was an exception, and Marcus opened the correct door immediately the bell rang. He had obviously been waiting for someone to call. He looked desperately anxious and I thought I detected the trace of a tear on his cheek. Something had clearly upset him a very great deal.

"Whatever is the matter?" I exclaimed.

He answered in his thick Scottish accent:

"I am so pleased to see you. I've been robbed during the night. I cannot believe this has happened to me. Can you imagine how anyone could be so despicable as to target a poor man like myself?"

To say that I was alarmed would be an understatement. I asked him whether he had called the police, to which he answered in the negative. I looked around the house and could find no signs of forced entry, and there appeared to be nothing missing. Even his wallet sat on his bedside table and I could see quite clearly that it contained a quantity of cash. I asked him if there was anything missing prior to my phoning the office and the police.

"Yes," he replied. "Some nasty crook has had my teeth away."

I managed to stifle a giggle as I realised what must have happened. He had taken out his dentures the night before and forgotten where he had put them. I had experienced this before with other things lost, and had learnt to look in the most unlikely places first. Last time it was his glasses, and he had failed to look in the mirror to see that he was actually wearing them. Some time ago he had lost his hearing aids. I found them in the toilet, which, thank goodness, he had failed to flush. They had needed a thorough clean and then everything was okay.

Firstly I looked in his mouth, to see if he actually had them in situ. He hadn't, so I began the search of the most unlikely places. I checked the microwave, cereal box, fridge, toilet, cake tin, etc., etc. No teeth! Eventually I found them in the freezer, thawed them out and reassured him that there had been no burglary.

I was just about to get his breakfast when the doorbell rang and I was very surprised to see Colin waiting on the doorstep.

"Whatever are you doing here today?" I asked. "It's on my timesheet to come to Marcus on a Wednesday."

"The office phoned me yesterday," he replied, "and asked me to cover your morning calls as you had an important meeting this morning."

"It's news to me," I replied. "I know nothing of any meeting."

I phoned the office with some trepidation. Whatever had happened to cause me to be recalled to the office with no notice?! I was surely going to get my P45 for some ridiculous error I had made some time ago. Was it a breach of some company policy, or a lack of care leading to a serious health and safety issue? Had I eventually been found out for becoming too friendly with my many clients? It is at times like these that the mind goes into overdrive, causing one to go over the past few months in the same manner that one would re-live their life just before certain death.

In a haze of uncertainty I became aware that the phone had been answered.

"Hello, Charlotte here. How can I help?"

"Chris returning your call! [I'd forgotten that there had been no call!] Whatever is the matter? I seem to have clashed with Colin and have been told that I am due for a meeting in the office. I know nothing about this."

"Interview!" exclaimed Charlotte. "Why are you not present for the interview for the post of senior care assistant?"

"Because I didn't realise there was an interview today," I replied. "No one told me to attend so I haven't got it in my diary!"

"Well, please turn up for an interview now! You have filled in the application form and we are doing the interviews today, so please turn up as soon as possible. All care calls have been transferred to Colin for the day."

I rang off with mixed feelings of excitement and trepidation. I remembered that I had completed an application form for a more senior post, but assumed that my age would exclude me from any real possibility of actually gaining promotion. I had put the whole idea firmly to the back of my mind and assumed that I was to spend the rest of my working life as a simple care assistant. I hadn't even thought of preparing for such an event, and it had been a long time since I had undergone an interview process.

I duly turned up at the office, having warned them that I was unprepared for an interview, and was cross-questioned in my usual care worker attire, i.e. no tie or jacket, purely a functional clothing mode that spoke volumes about care work but very little about management.

To my astonishment I got the job and soon became used to the fact that I was now referred to as a senior support worker. It was pointed out to me that I had to undertake a serious risk assessment and health and safety training session somewhere in Devon and that, once accredited, I would be expected to carry out assessments in people's homes.

I later learned that I was to be offered the post of senior support worker for eleven hours a week. After those hours I would revert to the title of support worker and never the twain shall meet. In other words, I had been promoted, but only for eleven hours a week. Anything beyond those hours was to be considered at the lower pay rate. I was also expected to take part in the 'on-call' rota, which meant being available for problems outside office hours and being able to deal with those problems immediately and without question.

I felt slightly foolish that I may have accepted a 'poisoned chalice' of a job, by increasing my responsibility whilst distancing myself from those I really cared about, for not much more pay.

I looked forward to my extra training with anticipation of new things to come and secretly wondered what new delights would come my way after I had become a fully qualified risk assessor.

21st February 2008
The Brigadier

Today I am on my own! Having undergone extensive risk assessment training and 'in the field' supervision, I am now considered to be a fully qualified senior support worker. Alone, I am trying to put together an individual service plan for The Brigadier. I have to say that I feel a little apprehensive, despite the long hours of training in inspection and the filling in of such lengthy and bureaucratic forms. I have been trained in health and safety, risk assessment, ISPs (individual service plans), customer relations, company policies, care standards, care legislation and a raft of other requirements of a senior support worker. I have also been shadowed by my immediate line manager, who has deemed that I am now fit to be unleashed on the unsuspecting public. What could possibly go wrong?

Nothing could have prepared me for this first assignment, a home visit to The Brigadier. I approached the imposing thatched cottage with some fear and trembling, having been forewarned that The Brigadier was a formidable character and one that didn't suffer fools gladly. I had been informed that his full title was Brigadier Prothero-White and that he liked formality to be maintained at all times. Knowing that military gentlemen of his stature were sticklers for punctuality, I arrived at precisely the stated time of 12.30pm and rang the imposing doorbell pull cord. The door was answered, as I had predicted, by a housekeeper, who informed me that I was expected and that The Brigadier would see me in the study.

Having found myself in the study after a considerable walk and been formally introduced to The Brigadier, I was asked to sit.

"I trust that you understand that, whilst the body may be getting a little weak, the mind is as acute as ever," The Brigadier stated unnecessarily, as I could see that he was fully aware of his present situation. Whilst he had gained a considerable stoop through age and infirmity, he still conveyed a total military bearing and seemed to stand to some sort of bent attention, despite his evident lack of erectness.

"You will understand that I expect my life to be conducted with military precision. Everything ordered and in its place, don't you know? And everything done to a strict timetable, don't you know? I expect any person who enters this house to respect my way of life and to have total regard for my routine, don't you know?"

"Of course, Brigadier, and I do know," I answered, rather sheepishly, accepting my somewhat lower status in life in the presence of such a larger than life military character. "I am so sorry to impose on your busy life but, according to the care standards, I do have to fill in this rather tedious form. I will be asking you some rather strange questions, which you may decline to answer, but I assure you that every question is necessary as far as the Commission for Social Care Inspectorate is concerned. I will then need to undertake a health and safety inspection of your beautiful cottage and assess your mobility capabilities."

He looked extremely cross, and I had a strong feeling that he was about to explode into a tirade of verbal abuse against me for daring to even suggest that his life may need some sort of assessment. I had to act quickly and diffuse the situation.

"You will understand, as a prominent military gentleman, that I have to follow orders and that, however silly those orders may seem, I still have to obey, without question or argument."

His expression visibly softened and he seemed to warm to me as he replied:

"I can tell that you are a man of principle, and I would be happy to hear your questions, though doubt whether I will be prepared to answer them. As far as inspections of my home are concerned, I would require more explanation, as it seems to imply that I am not running a safe house."

"We have a duty of care to our staff, under the Health and Safety at Work Act," I replied. I was going to include the date of the act but felt it a little unnecessary at the present time. I felt sure that he would know of the existence of such an act, even if it didn't apply to the safety of soldiers that might have been under his command in the past.

"I have to ensure that there are no hazards, such as frayed carpets, trailing wires, dodgy electrical appliances, etc. If I don't warn staff of such hazards I would be failing in my job and I could lay my organisation open to litigation if anyone got hurt whilst on duty. I also need to assure myself that you are safe from harm whilst my staff are discharging their duties."

"I understand fully; please carry on, and make it snappy," The Brigadier replied.

"Please could I have your full name, Brigadier?"

"Brigadier Christopher Henry Montague Bellenden Prothero-White!" came the snappy reply. I found that I didn't have enough space to put such a long name on the form and stupidly left off the 'Brigadier' at the start of the name. I had never come across such a long name before.

"And how would you like to be addressed?" I continued.

"And just what the hell do you mean by that question?" he replied.

"Well, it means what would you like to be called by the care assistants who may come to help you? Would you prefer to be called Christopher, Chris, Mr Prothero or Brigadier Prothero–White without any Christian names? I do need to know as I would hate to cause any offence."

"I am known as The Brigadier and that is what I am, so I would be grateful for the courtesy of being called by my proper title. Brigadier will do nicely, thank you. Next question."

"What is your religion?" I asked with some trepidation.

"What the hell business is that of yours?" he thundered.

"Well," I replied rather sheepishly, "I need to know, because some religions have certain customs that it would be wrong to ignore. For example, if you were of a certain religion, it would be wrong to send a female carer to look after your needs, as some faiths dictate that only the same sex may administer care."

"I fully understand, now that you have explained, and I am quite happy to tell you that I am Church of England and proud of it. I am therefore totally unconcerned about the gender of any carer who may come to help.

"I must, however, ask whether it would be required of me to wear swimming trunks should a future carer be female, so as to hide my obvious masculinity. I would hate to cause offence by exposing those bits and pieces that may offend the opposite sex!"

"Please don't worry," I replied, warming to his sense of dignity. "Our care assistants are well used to dealing with personal care and would not require you to 'cover up' during the course of a visit. I understand your concern and would advise you to do whatever you feel comfortable with, but I assure you that our female care assistants are not at all fazed by the sight of male bits and pieces."

"Very well, then," replied The Brigadier. I will play this according to your advice."

The next question seemed mundane, but caused problems equal to the one before. The only way I can put this down is to record the conversation exactly and to prefix each exchange with the name of the person so speaking, i.e. Me being me and Brig. being The Brigadier:

Me – "And do you have a named key holder to your cottage?"

Brig. – "My housekeeper and gardener both hold keys to this cottage."

Me – "Could I please have their names?"

Brig. – "My housekeeper is called Mildred and my gardener is called Jones."

Me – "And what are their surnames?"

Brig. – "Good gracious me! I am not aware of the surname of my housekeeper; and Jones is the surname of my gardener, and I have no idea of his Christian name. Why would I ever need to know this information?"

Me – " Because I require it for my form."

Brig. – "Well, you can carefully stuff your form in an appropriate place, as I don't know the answer. I expect you will be asking me where they live next."

Me – "Since you ask, I do need to know their addresses."

Brig. – "And why in heaven's name would one need to know the address of one's housekeeper or gardener? I have their phone numbers and their names. Whatever else do I need? They have worked for me for the past eighteen years and I have never needed to know where they lived. I am hardly likely to want to call on them socially."

Me – "I need the information to comply with the care standards and to make sure we know how to access your property should you experience a fall and not be able to answer the door. If it causes you some problem to give me their addresses, I would be quite happy to put down their phone numbers."

"Wait a moment, I seem to remember that Mildred was known as Mildred Taylor," he said, just as I was beginning to despair.

He gave me the numbers and I looked them up in the telephone directory and, from the electoral roll, it transpired that his housekeeper lived six doors away and his gardener lived in the next road.

After eighteen years he had failed to acknowledge that his hired help lived in close proximity to him, and he still gave orders over the phone.

I spoke to both of his servants at a later date and they both expressed extreme loyalty to The Brigadier; and I have to admit that, despite his pompousness, I have grown to respect him as a truly larger than life character and someone who enriches the lives of us lesser mortals. Long live The Brigadier!

As a senior support worker, the care assistants often spoke to me of their amusing stories of what had occurred during the course of their work.

One lady reported back to me on her first visit to The Brigadier. Her task was to give him a bath or shower. It was obvious that he was still concerned about appearing totally naked in front of a strange female. However, he laughed this off by saying:

"Don't worry! I even find it hard to raise a smile these days!"

Another interesting thing happened to a more mature female carer who went to visit Paul Pickering, aged eighty-five years. He was known to be an absolute charmer to the ladies, and when she arrived he asked her how old she was. She replied that she was fifty years old. He then said:

"Well, you look as if you're in your mid-30s, and very attractive at that."

Feeling a little elated at this she decided she needed to know more and looked at the care plan. In large print it stated that Paul was registered blind! Coming back down to earth she realised why he had a white stick by his side.

17th March 2008

Toby, the sex fiend

Today I have been reminded that anything can happen to a senior support worker, just as it invariably happens to a support worker. Promotion does nothing to prevent us from being exposed to embarrassing situations that, in hindsight, can be very amusing. It has been some weeks since my memorable encounter with The Brigadier, and I am due for something unusual to happen again.

I have been instructed to do an individual service plan for a Mrs Sybil Bewdley and have duly arrived at an imposing block of flats in sedate Branksome Park. My notes tell me that Mrs Bewdley has been in hospital having suffered a mild stroke that has affected her left-hand side and her mobility. We are to attend to her care for an hour every morning, beginning next week.

I rang the entry intercom, which was answered by a lady, who asked me to enter and warned me that she had a rather lively dog. She added that if I stood very still, he would soon settle down. I arrived at the front door of the first-floor flat and gingerly pressed the doorbell, to be met with what could only be described as a cacophony of canine noise. A very strikingly beautiful young lady answered the door and let loose a whirlwind of black, curly dog that immediately latched itself on to my right leg with its front paws and tried to commit some sort of obscene act with my shin. I don't know what it is about my legs, but they do seem to be terribly attractive to small dogs. Perhaps I should change my soap! On closer inspection I noted that the dog was a toy poodle, and further made a mental note to ensure that only dog-friendly carers be sent to this address.

"Don't mind Toby," she said. "He'll soon settle down."

Which he did, almost immediately. I breathed a sigh of relief that must have been noticeable, as the young lady apologised for her dog's unseemly behaviour.

"I'm so sorry about Toby. He just seems to like the men and doesn't do this to the ladies."

Another mental note, to tone down my previous note about dog-friendly carers, just as long as they were female. I also wondered why a male dog seemed to want to mate with male humans, and assumed that he must have some sort of hang-up with his sexuality.

"My name is Samantha, but you may call me Sam. I'm afraid that Mummy is still in hospital, but we can do all the necessary paperwork so that you can supply care as soon as she is discharged."

"I do need to see your mother to assess her mobility, so I can carry out some of the service plan now but will have to make a hospital visit," I replied.

I then went through the usual questions about age, next of kin, religion, ethnicity, any illnesses, allergies, medication, and everything seemed to be going fine until I explained that I had to carry out a health and safety check, to ensure that there were no identifiable risks to Mrs Bewdley or to our staff. I made the mistake of standing up too fast, which created another frenzy of sexual activity from Toby. This dog certainly had stamina!

The dog then followed us from room to room as I checked a kettle here, an electric fire there and rugs and carpets everywhere. Every time I stopped, Toby would look up at me with his crazily seductive eyes, as if imploring me to give him some special attention.

Samantha seemed oblivious to his antics, until we arrived at a bedroom the likes of which I had never seen before. The whole room was decorated like a scene from the Hundred Acre Wood, and on a huge, mega king-sized bed were equally huge soft toys in the form of Winnie the Pooh, Tigger, Eeyore, Piglet and a rabbit whose name I forget. I half expected to see Christopher Robin arrive through the door, which was shaped like a huge entrance to a beehive.

"Sorry about the strange taste in décor," said Sam, with a slight note of humour in her tone as she saw my utter astonishment at the sight before me. "This was my room when I lived here. I was a great fan of AA Milne and insisted that everything was done with a Winnie theme."

She then physically turned me so that I was facing away from the bed, but I could see Toby out of the corner of my eye jumping on the bed as I turned. What Samantha didn't realise was that she had turned me into a position directly in front of a large mirror which gave me a splendid view of the disgraceful antics unfolding behind me. Toby was firmly attached to Winnie the Pooh and was attempting to mate with him. When the amorous advance met with no response, he turned his attention to Eeyore, thence to Tigger and Piglet!

By the time he got the rabbit whose name I forget he began to slow in his performance and soon lay on his back, panting, looking absolutely shattered. It was then that Sam, looking into my astonished face, remembered the mirror and blushed to the deepest shade of purple that I have ever seen on such a lovely face.

"I'm so sorry," she exclaimed. "He seems to get turned on by the sight of Winnie the Pooh!"

You could say that, I was about to say, but felt that a little silence at such a sensitive time was the best option. I made my excuses and left, to go to the hospital to meet Mum. However, this little episode reminded me that we never know what is around the corner, like the time when I visited Gregory whilst still a humble care assistant last year.

4th February 2007
Bang, bang

The sound was loud! Deafeningly loud! It occurred as I stood at the slightly ajar front door of a new client's house. It was obvious that the gunshot had come from inside. Then I heard the words, "Tell me where you keep the money or I'll blow you to pieces!!" I felt that my new client must be in imminent danger but knew that if I made my presence felt, I too could be in danger. It also struck me that the door was open, while I had been told that there was a key safe. I looked at the safe and saw that it was wide open and there was no sign of a key.

I needed to call the police but found that I had left my mobile in the car. As I headed for the car my thoughts immediately turned to the circumstances and reasons for my call to Mr Gregory Black and the instructions that I had received that very morning.

Mr Gregory Black is suffering from dementia. He needs help to get up in the morning, prompt medication and to prepare breakfast. Mr Black is a little deaf and needs to be observed at all times to ensure he has carried out all of his personal care tasks. He keeps a rather noisy parrot and has a keen interest in his garden and allotment. He forgets easily and won't answer the doorbell. Use the key safe and shout a greeting before you enter the lounge, as he is likely to be startled by a sudden appearance, as will the parrot.

I reached the car in seconds that seemed to be hours, grabbed my mobile and was about to dial 999 when I heard the distinctive voice of my old friend, Darren the Postie.

"Whatever is the matter, Chris?" he said, and added, "You look to be in a state of shock!"

"I have come to see Mr Black and I heard a gunshot and a threat of extreme violence from within the house. I am calling the police as I really fear for his safety."

"I wouldn't do that if I were you. I know Gregory well and also know that he likes to watch old gangster movies at this time of the morning. He has the television on very loud so he can hear it. You are clearly hearing the television."

What a relief that was. I thanked Darren, feeling rather foolish, and headed back to the house. I quietly entered the hall and shouted:

"Hello! It's Chris from the care agency!"

The only response I got was the sound of two more shots and a squawking parrot. I entered the lounge and was greeted by the parrot that said in his parrot voice, *"Are you the vicar?"*

The parrot obviously acted as an alarm system, as Gregory immediately turned round to be confronted with a stranger in his lounge. He seemed somewhat alarmed and had obviously forgotten that I was calling today. He stood up to attention. He had a row of medals on his chest and stated in a quick-fire military manner:

"7911502! Private Black! SIR!"

"Stand easy," I said, remembering my days in the Air Training Corps and feeling that an old soldier deserved respect. "Is everything okay?" I asked, feeling that his military presence demanded a polite response.

He had an impressive row of medals attached to his jumper, which, on closer inspection, turned out to be medals for his horticulture and bird keeping skills. It appeared that he had been a prizewinner for carrots, parsnips, sprouts, sweet peas, budgerigars, canaries and parrots. As he turned off the television he replied:

"7911502! Private Black, SIR! Yes, everything is fine, but who in the hell are you?!"

*"Who are you? Who are you?" squawked the parrot. "Are you the vicar? Well, f*** off! Cheerio! Cheerio!" the parrot repeated.*

"Sorry, Mr Black, and Polly whatever your name is. I am from the care agency and I have come to help you with your morning tasks. I see that you are already up and dressed. Have you washed or showered and had breakfast?"

"I've had a raw carrot and a banana, and I have fed Ivor," he said, pointing to the noisy parrot. "But I could do with something else. Maybe a bacon butty."

I prepared the butty and we sat talking for the rest of my time there. He was most interesting and told me that he used to breed and sell exotic birds, and showed me what remained of his aviary. Now all he had was Ivor the parrot that he clearly loved. He also explained that his nephew lived with him but left very early in the morning for his work.

I visited Gregory for some months, but had to finish the visits when I was promoted to senior support worker. However, I did speak to him again in different circumstances. I was on-call and the phone rang very early in the morning.

"Hello, is that Chris?" he sounded panicky and spoke with a very shaky voice. "My fire alarm is going off and I'm afraid the house might be on fire!"

"Can you see smoke or smell burning?" I asked, feeling somewhat uneasy.

Not wanting to panic him even more, I said that I would call the fire brigade, and advised him to put on a warm coat and go outside as a precaution. I hung up and dialled 999.

I got the usual response of asking which emergency service I required. I said fire and was put through to fire control. I knew the workings of the control through my membership of the Fire Authority, and I knew most of the staff. I told them that I worked for a care agency and that the occupant of a Poole address had called me rather than dialling 999 himself. I explained that he had dementia and that this might be a false alarm with good intent, but gave them the address and the name of the occupant and said that there might be another occupant in the house, namely his nephew, though he might be away. I just knew that they would take this seriously and would deploy fire fighters to this address as soon as they could.

I waited for some time and then rang fire control to find out what had happened. They told me that the alarm was due to a faulty smoke detector. They assured me that Gregory was fine and had gone back to bed. They had fitted a new smoke alarm, made him a cup of tea and had had a long chat with him. It transpired that his nephew had gone to sleep with his radio on and his earphones firmly attached to his ears. The whole situation had passed him by.

They also spoke of a strange bird in the lounge that was most unwelcoming and kept saying, rather rudely, that he wanted them to leave and that he would prefer the company of the vicar! We all laughed, and I thanked them for their trouble. I was able to report to the fire chief that he had a really professional set of fire fighters in Poole who took the trouble to perform their duties with a very real compassion that went beyond their usual tasks.

4th July 2007

A game of cat and mouse

After my visits to Toby the dog and Ivor the parrot, I remembered the times when I had had other meetings with service users' pets. Apart from Timmy the tortoise, cats, dogs, parrots and a budgerigar, I had had some serious times with chickens and a huge tomcat. Firstly, I will relate the cat incident.

Pam and Noel Laithwaite are a truly great couple. Both are severely disabled, with Noel having a debilitating disability that he unfortunately had at birth, although he never complained and had clearly learned from a very young age to live with his problems and just get on with life. Pam suffered from polio as a child and was quite mobile when I first knew her, but unfortunately she now suffers from post-polio, which means that she is now confined to a wheelchair.

Some years ago I first visited them in their small bungalow to assist Noel and was immediately struck by his determination in very difficult circumstances. Their home was most unsuitable for their disabilities, with narrow doorways and tight corners. However, they coped as best they could, helped by their two lovely cats, Polly and Molly. Polly was Molly's mum, and they were great company and considered part of their family.

I was most concerned about their accommodation and, as a local councillor, determined to help them find a more suitable home. After some time, we managed to find a housing association ground floor flat in the centre of Poole. After much searching and heartache I had finally found a potential home. It was still in the process of being built, so it was possible to design the interior especially with their disabilities in mind.

After some time the flat was ready for them to move into, when they received the devastating news that pets were not permitted on the estate. Being a believer that pets can be tremendously therapeutic to the more vulnerable amongst us, I determined to fight this unreasonable ruling with any means possible, especially as Polly and Molly were house cats and never ventured outside.

My first idea proved to be the right one. I phoned Southern Television and explained the situation and the reasons why I felt that Pam and Noel were being discriminated against. Within an hour a camera crew arrived at their bungalow and interviewed them.

The crew then descended on the newly built estate to question residents and, to their surprise, found dogs and cats aplenty. It seemed that not everyone was following the rules. By the time the situation aired on the evening news, the association had announced that it had rescinded the rule, and Pam and Noel were able to move to their new home, together with their beloved cats.

I still come across situations where tenants have to abide by regulations that would not apply to homeowners. It would sometimes appear that vulnerable people could sometimes be treated as second-class citizens, something that flies in the face of the old adage that 'an Englishman's home is his castle'. It probably is, unless you are less fortunate and cannot afford to buy a hugely expensive dwelling.

I continued to visit Noel and Pat on an almost daily basis and always got a good greeting from their cats. Every

Wednesday I would go round before lunch to help them with the housework, and on this particular day I was in for a surprise.

I found the door locked and heard Noel trying to put the cats behind a closed door. This was unusual, as the cats never tried to get out. When the cats were safely put away Noel opened the door and a very worried couple greeted me. Something was clearly wrong. I asked what had happened and Pam said:

"You're never going to believe this, but as we opened the door earlier, for the postman, a most enormous tomcat pushed his way into our flat and is now sitting on top of the kitchen cabinet looking very cross. We don't know how to get rid of him, and he has been chasing Polly and Molly in an attempt to mate with them. At least we have now been able to shut them out of harm's way."

I made my way to the kitchen and found a very cross-looking cat that could only be described as very large. He glowered at me with his huge eyes, and I felt at that moment like a frightened mouse. I felt sure that if he leapt at me he could inflict some serious damage with his razor-sharp teeth. He seemed to be looking directly at my neck as though concentrating on the area of my jugular!

"Here kitty, kitty," I said in a faltering voice, not convinced that he would take my advice. He looked even crosser, so I grabbed a tea tray to use as a shield. With the tray protecting my face, I armed myself with a large wooden spoon in order to tap the monster's bottom and get him to come down to my level. On the first tap it was clear that he wasn't going to budge so, knowing that cats have a serious aversion to water, I threw a glass of the liquid at the stubborn animal, making him jump from the cabinet with a loud screech. He then arched his back, tail erect and mouth wide open with a noisy scowl, and glared at me as if to attack. I was determined that I wasn't going to be beaten by a cat.

There then ensued a chase around the flat. I was still armed with a wooden spoon, as we played a serious game of cat and mouse. Sometimes I was ahead of the game, only to have the roles reversed whenever I got him into a tight corner. I had to use the tea tray shield on a number of occasions as he made desperate efforts to thwart me.

In the meantime Pam and Noel were not taking the situation as seriously as before and both couldn't contain their mirth at me chasing and being chased by a large cat. To say they were roaring with laughter would be an understatement. I was just glad that they were laughing so much that they didn't think to get a camera to record my antics. However, I ignored their laughs, just grateful that there was no record to share with my workmates.

Eventually I cornered the beast on the windowsill and managed to open the window before he realised what was about to happen. I then thrust the offending monster out of the window with the wooden spoon and sent him tumbling and screeching to the path below. Believing that he would be waiting for me when I left, I stayed in the safety of the flat for over an hour, completing my housework chores and reassuring Polly and Molly that all was back to normal.

I then had to go to the next client, and made a dash for the car. The beast had gone, or so I thought. As I drove away I caught a glimpse of a huge cat in pursuit of his aggressor. He had obviously been hiding amongst the rubbish bins. I made my escape at some speed and thankfully never saw the cat again. I assume that someone had somehow put an end to his reign of terror.

Polly and Molly seemed to sense that I had somehow saved their innocence, and always gave me a good greeting whenever

I arrived at their home. I still visit Pam, although Noel has sadly passed away. Once again I am pleased to say that a friend has left a huge legacy of love and understanding, and people who knew him remember him with great affection. He never complained about his lot and inspired others to look at life in a way that improved their outlook and also helped them to help others. Farewell, Noel, and rest in peace knowing that you have left a lasting legacy that will endure for many years.

It would be very remiss of me not to mention Pam and her continued stoicism. She will never get over the loss of her dear husband, but will continue his work in helping people to understand that disability doesn't make anyone different, only more understanding.

I will always try to help those who seek my assistance, but one day in 2007 made me wonder whether I had done the right thing in agreeing to look after someone's chickens.

15th August 2007

I am the egg man!

Today I have had a rather unusual request from the wife of one of my clients. Thomas Merchant has gone into respite care to give his wife Cynthia a more than welcome break. Tom and Cynthia live on the edge of a very sleepy Dorset town and reside happily in a charming bungalow surrounded by fields with far-reaching views of the Purbeck Hills. They are passionate about growing and nurturing all that they may need to sustain their healthy lifestyles. Tom can't do too much anymore due to his multiple sclerosis, but supports Cynthia in any way that he can. However, I digress.

Today I have been asked to perform the simple task of gathering the eggs from their small flock of chickens, and to make sure that they are secure for the night in their cosy chicken coop, to keep them safe from night-time predators. It is only for one night and I feel confident that I can cope, having watched the process on a number of occasions. At least it will give Cynthia a chance to spend the night with her sister.

I duly arrived at their idyllic home well before nightfall, to enable me to collect the results of the day's egg laying and transfer them to their kitchen. I approached the chicken run with confidence, but stupidly forgot to take any sort of container. On opening the gate to the chicken run I became aware that the hens were somewhat agitated by my presence.

It seemed that they were looking suspiciously at me as if I were a hungry fox. The squawk of one hen is enough to put anyone off their stride, but the cacophony of a dozen hens squawking is somewhat alarming. However, I proceeded into the enclosure, albeit a little less confidently than before.

As I approached the henhouse to collect the eggs I became aware that I was being hotly pursued by a number of hens that seemed intent on pecking my heels. Reaching the safety of the henhouse, I looked for the result of the day's egg laying and was more than surprised to find over a dozen lying at various places within the straw.

Without a container I gathered a handful and proceeded outside. I was met with a ferocious chase across the chicken run and managed to save only three eggs from destruction as I avoided the obvious anger from the hens. I had to go back and complete my task and seemed to annoy my chicken friends even more as I tried to make my way back to the henhouse to collect the remaining eggs. This time I had taken a suitable container and managed to retrieve all of the remaining eggs and place them in the kitchen, after much chasing and pecking.

The only thing that remained was to get the chickens into the henhouse for the night, something they clearly didn't want to do. I armed myself with a very large piece of cardboard, to be used as a guidance device, and tried to get a dozen hens into one group, whereby I could shepherd them into the henhouse. I spoke to them in a stern voice, warning them of the dangers of staying out all night, particularly from Mr Fox.

They took absolutely no notice and the chase that ensued was two-sided. On the one side I was chased across the run by very angry looking hens, and on the other side I managed to get them into some semblance of order and eventually, after more than two hours, got them all into the henhouse for the night.

A task that should have taken a half hour had taken three hours, and I ended up completing the task well into the ensuing nightfall.

The following day I was much relieved to see Cynthia, apart from her comments that she was disappointed about the egg production of the previous day. Needless to say, I didn't pass comment and she never knew that some eggs had met their end by crashing to the floor before they arrived in the kitchen.

However, the eggs that were left were offered to me as a thank-you gift for my efforts. I warmly received them, as I knew that they had been freshly laid and had rich, tasty yolks. My family would be richly rewarded for my efforts in hen control when they enjoyed boiled eggs for breakfast the next morning.

I have come across many instances when I have become the receiver of gifts of produce, as many of my clients, or their families, lovingly tended their allotments, vegetable patches or greenhouses.

16th July 2006
Courgettes and tomatoes

When administering care in as professional manner as possible, one becomes part of the family scene of the service user. This means that support workers tend to become friends and a part of the family situation.

In effect, we become friends rather than employees of a care organisation. It is for this reason that we get offered some of the produce of their allotments or vegetable patches.

I well remember such a family, whose daughter, Faith, was looking after her very aged and infirm father. Her partner Gwendolyn successfully ran her own allotment, where she produced the most amazing vegetables. The only problem was that she would produce so much that they couldn't cope with the quantity. It is always the case that home-grown produce appears at a time when the same produce is cheapest in the shops because they are in season.

However, Gwen produced some fine specimens of vegetables and brought home some impressive courgettes, almost the size of marrows. These she would proceed to give to me, and they were gratefully received. However, the sheer quantity of marrow-sized courgettes meant that I had to give most of them to neighbours and friends. The same applied to cabbages, beans, peas, cauliflowers, spinach and tomatoes.

It was the tomatoes that really got to me. There were so many that I had to implore my wife to try to make chutney and tomato sauce. Every morning I received a new bag of freshly picked tomatoes at a time when the local supermarkets were selling at their lowest price levels of the year. I soon became a tomato benefactor, as I was receiving them regularly from at least eight sources and found I had to give most of them away to unsuspecting clients who didn't have gardens, or to the care workforce. We may have been on very low wages as care workers, but during the summer months we were certainly not short of vegetables.

15th June 2006

How does your garden grow?

Having received more than my fair share of courgettes and tomatoes, I am reminded of visits to clients when more than care was on the agenda. This usually involved strange requests, or furtive gifts of sweets and garden produce. Every week I went to visit Isobel Morris, who liked to be addressed as Izzy. Unfortunately she suffered from multiple sclerosis, and my task was to keep her company for three hours whilst her full-time carer had a break. Her illness was quite advanced and she suffered bouts of extreme pain, especially in her legs. She was about to undergo a surgical procedure to remove nerves in her legs. This would mean that she would not be able to move her legs anymore, but she felt it was preferable to the pain she suffered.

Izzy had good and bad days and shunned too much medication, preferring to use alternative therapies. It was during my visit today that I came across one of her homemade, or home-grown, remedies. When I arrived on this beautiful sunny morning I was advised that she was in the back garden. I found her happily singing away with a large-handled fork in her hand, trying to do some weeding from her wheelchair. I offered to help, although gardening was not on our list of ‘can do’ tasks. She asked me to look behind a piece of fencing that seemed to be in a border with no real purpose. It wasn't until I looked behind the fence that I realised the purpose of it.

In a piece of land about twelve feet square stood a hearty crop of cannabis plants. She explained that she used the cannabis to alleviate the pain and to give her a much-needed lift. She pointed to the garden shed and inside was another batch, drying out and almost ready for use. She said that getting supplies on the illegal market was difficult so she had decided to grow it for herself. The strange smell in the house that I sometimes encountered began to make sense.

I had also noticed that she seemed far happier whenever the smell was around, although I never saw her smoking.

Now I was in a quandary. Something illegal was occurring in a client's property and I should inform the office in order to cover myself. However, when she explained the situation to me I felt that I had to maintain the trust I had built up over the years. It transpired that a medical practitioner had expressed concern that this illegal drug could not be provided on the National Health, even though it was quite clear that its use alleviated suffering from this incurable disease.

I told her that I would keep her secret but would not join her in a 'joint', as I felt sure that that would be against regulations. I had only smoked cannabis once in my life, when a joint was passed around at a student party when I was at college. I was disappointed that everyone but me seemed to be getting high, whilst I was turning a shade of green and felt very dizzy. I never tried it again and was not about to start now.

Now when I sit with Izzy, she smokes the weed quite openly, and I have to say that it does make her much better company. I don't know what happened to her, as I had to stop the visits when I became a team leader, but I did warn the new support worker that she might find something a little out of the ordinary during her visits.

15th May 2008
The wrath descends

Today will not go down as the best of days in my career as a senior support worker. I have just had a disastrous morning call to the highly religious Potter family and am acutely aware that I have upset them and their high religious principles to such an extent that I will never be welcome in their house again.

I must point out at this stage that their firmly held beliefs meant that they shunned alcohol, tobacco, extravagance and any use or reference to profanity or the utterance of any swear word. I never cease to be amazed that one small mistake can have such horrendous consequences that can potentially damage one's career and future life. This time I have really blown it, as there is bound to be an inquiry into my behaviour and some disciplinary action taken, which could result in the sack.

I have always got on well with the extended Potter clan and gone along with their rather extreme religious tendencies, despite my own rather vague beliefs. I had always been taught to avoid all topics religious or political, and I never discussed these subjects with the Potters. I merely listened and obeyed. This meant closing my eyes whilst the family were praying, putting my hands together when required and saying 'Amen' at the appropriate times. My observance of their customs had assured me of invitations to all of their family gatherings, and I considered that I had become a family friend.

Family gatherings were always conducted in the quietest of manners by all involved. They were always opened with prayers and followed by polite conversation that usually revolved around the meaning of life and the terrible state of the world today. I always left with the feeling that the end of the world was nigh and that most of us would be condemned to an afterlife of doom, gloom and sackcloth and ashes.

I well remember attending such an event last Christmas. Mr Tobias Potter was in bed as usual, suffering from his acute illness, while his wife Elsie recited prayers. All of the grown-up Potter children, of which there were seven, sat in sober silence, listening to the words of their mother. Only two of the children had married, and I assumed that the lack of grandchildren was due to the fact that the subject of sex was taboo in this household and had probably never been performed by any of the children. I often secretly marvelled at the hypocrisy that enabled the mother and father to produce seven children yet taught that sex was somehow dirty and evil. They must have been at it like rabbits during their early marriage.

Following prayers, the family and I formed a circle to have a discussion about the commercialisation of Christmas and the fact that the true meaning was now all but forgotten by many families. I had to agree to a certain point, but secretly yearned after my own home at this time, with the excessive Yuletide decorations, huge tree with many twinkling lights, bulging fridge and drinks cabinet, and popular Christmas music playing throughout the house.

The Potters home was, by comparison, dismal. A six-inch-high tinsel tree stood on the windowsill, devoid of any decoration. Twelve cards were on the mantelpiece, and the only concession to Christmas festivities was a tin of boiled sweets on the table. There was no television or music player, as such equipment was thought to be the product of the devil. The only sign of modern technology was an elderly wireless that was put on only for religious programmes and the news. I made my apologies and got up to leave.

"Please stay for another drink," Elsie pleaded. "We are having such fun, and it would be a pity for you to miss the games and our nativity play."

I declined the drink; firstly as I was driving, and secondly because there is a limit to the amount of tea that anyone can drink in one afternoon. I really had no desire to see the Potter children perform the nativity play again. I had seen it the past two years and was less than impressed, and the games were tedious to say the least. I hadn't played 'put the tail on the donkey' whilst blindfolded since childhood, and 'spin the platter' was a definite no-no.

Which brings me back to today and what I have done to cause so much distress. I arrived at my usual time of 8.30am to administer a bed bath to Tobias. He was almost completely immobile, but was scrupulous about the cleanliness of both his body and soul. The ritual of washing was always preceded by a prayer, which was always said by Elsie, who would kneel by the bed with uplifted hands while Tobias bowed his head and I closed my eyes and bit my tongue.

"Heavenly Father, we thank Thee for delivering us all to another day and ask Thee to pour down Thy blessings on this household after Thee hast looked after all of those who cry out for Thy help in their hour of need. We ask that all those who don't believe, come to understand Your wisdom and truth and that, in so doing, the world will become a better place. We especially ask for guidance to carry us through this day and particularly ask that You bestow Your blessings on Christopher, and that his important work this morning be carried out well. Endow him with the skills to perform his tasks with Tobias and ensure a clean body and a tidy bedroom. Help him in his important works throughout this day and enable him to return safely to us tomorrow. We especially thank Thee for the continued life of Tobias and understand that his illness is but a trial for his life ahead of being at your side in the life hereafter. Bless the water that will be used for the washing and the soap that will be used for the cleaning, the towels that will be used for the drying and the clothes that will be used for the modesty. Above all, thank Thee for Thy patience and abiding love. Amen."

I opened my eyes as I muttered 'Amen' and waited for Elsie to get a bowl of warm water – which will have been blessed, along with the soap, towels and freshly laundered clothes. I always wondered whether the family had managed to drag themselves into the 21st century or whether their minds remained set in some ancient biblical time when thees and thys were part of normal conversation. However, I felt comforted that I was mentioned in the prayer, despite being called Christopher, which I hate, having always been known as Chris. Perhaps the Good Lord did help me through the days – except, that is, today.

I was quite used to washing Tobias and knew exactly how to manoeuvre him to enable me to clean even the most inaccessible places. My work had been helped recently by the installation of a hospital bed, which was an all-singing, all-dancing piece of electronic wizardry that obeyed my every command. It would raise and lower at the touch of a button and would tilt in any direction. I could raise the head, the feet, the knees, the bottom and the back, either separately or all together. This was particularly useful as the bedroom was very small, and the presence of Elsie to supervise my work made space very limited. The bowl of water had to be placed on the bed, as there was no room for a table. I always placed the bowl on a towel to stop water spilling on to the bedclothes, and was always careful to move the bowl away from any part of the bed that was likely to rise. This meant moving the bowl backwards and forwards as I proceeded with the process of washing. I got the usual instructions from Elsie:

"Make sure you wash behind the ears, dry the groin properly, use more soap, be sure to get in all the wrinkles." Etc.

The ringing phone distracted me, but Elsie leaving to answer it gave me the opportunity to speed up the washing process. I quickly lowered the head end of the bed and raised the feet to allow easy access to between the toes. In my hurry I had forgotten the bowl of soapy water and watched in stunned silence as Tobias gesticulated frantically to me. He was obviously aware of what was about to happen but couldn't seem to get the words out to warn me. I looked in the direction of his gesticulations just in time to see the bowl tilt to such a degree that an accident had become inevitable. Reaching out to prevent the fall only made matters worse, as I seemed to push the bowl towards Tobias's middle, causing the soapy water to cascade over both Mr Potter and the bed. I tried to correct the direction of the water but only succeeded in aiming the rest of the water at the floor and myself. In trying to escape this I accidentally kicked over the half-full urine bottle, spilling its contents to join the soapy water.

"Oh BUGGER!" I exclaimed, a little too loudly. The moment I uttered those words I knew my fate was sealed. The Potters simply didn't swear. My only hope was that they didn't understand what I had just said.

Mrs Potter entered the room looking somewhat stony faced. All she said was, "That was the minister on the phone. I would be grateful if you would clear up this mess and then leave." Mr Potter didn't look too pleased either, which I tended to understand.

She produced a mop, bucket and a lot of drying up cloths, and watched my efforts in a silence that was so intense it was almost deafening. I tried to apologise but my mutterings fell on deaf ears. When I had finished the task to her satisfaction I was shown the door and never saw the Potter family again. Their religion was certainly not a forgiving one.

Oh well, it was entirely my fault I suppose, and I wouldn't blame them if they made a serious official complaint about my behaviour. Such language is unforgiveable for someone in my position. I could only wait for the inevitable outcome.

To anyone who might be interested, I was withdrawn from the Potters the next morning and never received an explanation as to why, although I had a sneaky feeling I knew the answer. Needless to say, I kept quiet about the situation and never asked any questions to my employers. 'Least said, soonest mended!' is what my dear mother-in-law used to say to me whenever there was a potential problem. In this instance I had to agree with her.

24th June 2008
Onwards and upwards

Today is a very special day, as it has been decided that in our service the post of senior support worker will be axed and a new post of team leader will replace it. As a senior, I have the opportunity to apply for one of the three posts that will be available, but I must first show myself willing to undergo another qualification and the necessary training.

The new posts will be at a higher rate of pay; one full-time post will cover the Poole/Bournemouth conurbation; and the other two are part-time posts, one to cover Swanage, Wareham and the surrounding area, the other to cover the rest of Dorset. I am up for this and will do all that I can to secure the full-time post, as I am the only senior who actually lives in the conurbation. However, the others do appeal, as the sixteen-hour week would fit in nicely with my council commitments.

All three seniors have been accepted as future team leaders, subject to the necessary training being completed. My great work buddy Amanda has secured the Swanage post, which is sensible as she lives in Swanage. My other work pal Tracey has been placed in the full-time post responsible for Poole and Bournemouth – even though she lives in the heart of Dorset. She is, however, the most experienced. I have to take the only option left and accept the post of team leader for the rest of Dorset, which is a massive area with the least service users and care staff.

There then followed the training, which necessitated a weekly trip to Taunton. Amanda and I went together and shared the driving. Due to her experience, Tracey didn't attend, and I can only assume that she was far more advanced and qualified than us. However, we both passed with flying colours and proceeded to become dynamic team leaders for our respective areas.

So followed many months of travel around the four corners of deepest Dorset, and I have to admit that I was quite pleased to have drawn the short straw for the most widespread of the areas. I would often leave home in the morning with my first call being some fifty miles away, followed by one in some forgotten corner of the county. I would 'stagger' home, much refreshed by the delightful Dorset scenery, far too late to call into the office to report back. I was secretly grateful that I hadn't gained the conurbation post, which was, to say the least, full-on hard work. I did, however, help Tracey out when needed in that area as it really was too much for one person.

My time as team leader continued for some while, and I really enjoyed meeting so many rural souls and helping them to remain at their homes by providing care to help them. I had also been made Vice Chairman of the Dorset Fire Authority, so was able to get to know the many rural fire stations in Dorset.

However, sometimes the people needing help were so remote that I couldn't match them to support workers and had to pass them back to social services. They also had the same recruitment problem as myself, as there was a great dearth of available staff in remote areas. This was extremely negative, but the plus side was that I got to visit villages and settlements that I didn't even know existed. The place names conjured up images of times past, such as Toller Porcorum, Piddletrenthide, Tolpuddle, Puddletown, Ryme Intrinseca, etc.

I well remember my first call to some remote place. The lady concerned was ninety-nine years old and had requested help to do some tasks that she felt she could no longer cope with. I noticed that she walked without a stick and would get from place to place by holding on to strategically placed furniture. I asked whether she would like me to refer her to the occupational therapist to see if she could be supplied with some sort of walking aid. Her reply was typical of the gentlefolk of that generation.

"I am for too young to have need of that sort of help. I am only calling on you because I have reluctantly had to give up driving and sell the car. I need someone to take me to the shop in the nearest village that has one, which is ten miles away."

25th August 2008
The trouble with Bill

Today is a rather special day for me. Not only have I been promoted from senior support worker to team leader, I have begun to get an insight into the intricate workings of the brain of the impossible, irrepressible and eccentric William Treatham. It has been my absolute pleasure to have known Bill for over sixteen years, and I trust that he will excuse the use of the abbreviated Bill, instead of William, whilst I write of the extraordinary events that have filled my day today. The following story is in addition to my role as a carer, as I am acting as a friend rather than a care worker. It was not part of my remit to accompany Bill on his trips away from home, but he often called on my skills in care whenever he got into difficult situations.

I need to take due care and diligence over grammar in the next few pages in the knowledge that Bill is a stickler for correctness. He simply wouldn't excuse slapdash writing without the most genuine of excuses. My excuse is that I am writing in my diary, and no one is likely to read such obscure musings. However, if a publisher somehow got hold of these writings and decided to publish them, Bill would feel that he had to buy and read a copy. His disguised name might not be recognisable to him, but he would definitely remember the happenings of this day. Should anyone who knows him read this, they would also have an idea as to his true identity. Bill would be the first to laugh at himself and would chuckle over some of the pages, but he would also be the first to criticise bad grammar.

Bill, as I have said, was not one of my official charges but was a man of huge character and indeterminate age who I felt needed help and protection, as without that blanket of true care he was likely to get himself into unavoidable trouble. I accompanied him to the dentist, the doctor, and on delightful shopping trips and business engagements that would invariably leave memories that will linger in my mind for evermore.

One day he phoned me to ask whether I could accompany him to a specialist dentist in Southampton. This meant a simple train journey from Poole that was to end up as a hysterical day out. The fun started at Poole train station with a very bored-looking ticket man who knew, not how to smile, but how to annoy by his very presence. The conversation started as follows, with Bill starting:

"Could I please purchase two of your cheapest day return tickets?"

"Where would you like the return tickets to?" came the rather bored reply.

"Back here, of course," came the witty response from Bill.

Without a trace of a smile the ticket man replied:

"Yes, sir, but where are you going?"

"Well, it is my undoubted intention to travel back here, so that is where I would like my return tickets to go to in their inevitable eventuality. I am going from Poole and I want to return to Poole, for the simple reason that Poole is where I live, and I cannot understand why you may think that I may wish to return anywhere else. I do need to go to bed tonight so I need a return ticket back here and to nowhere else. Now, please furnish me with the required tickets."

The ticket man looked exasperated and I had the growing feeling that he was about to snap and throw us both out of the ticket hall. I knew that Bill was only joking and trying to wind the man up. I thought that I was going to have to intervene, when Bill got the clearest calm and measured response.

"Sir, I don't wish to seem unnecessarily tiresome," the dour man replied without even the slightest flicker of humour, "but I really need to have some idea as to your destination in order that I may issue the required tickets for you and your friend. I would point out that it is an offence under the relevant transportation and railway acts to travel without a current, and indeed correct, ticket and that if you were to board the said train without the proper authorisation in the form of a valid and fully paid-for travel document – that is one, or two, required and paid-for tickets – I would have no alternative but to inform the relevant authority – of the local ticket inspector or Transport Police – which regularly inspects and investigates on this particular line, that you are about to travel on illegally, unless you are in possession of a valid ticket. Do I make myself clear? Please, please tell me of your outward destination so that I may save you the embarrassment of any probable prosecution."

I was staggered by the ability of this man to produce such a statement without the need for a pause for breath. His lungs must have been of enormous capacity. I was also somewhat relieved to hear Bill's reply, and can only assume that he must have glanced behind and spotted the lengthening queue of very irritated-looking travellers. It had also been announced that the next train on Platform 1 was the 10.25am to Waterloo, stopping at Southampton.

"Save me from the officialdom," said Bill, "and sell me two return tickets to Poole via my intended visit to Southampton."

The angry man supplied the tickets, reluctantly, and with a huge sigh of relief from the fellow passengers. We boarded the train and were soon settled and on our way. We literally rattled through the next four stations, and on reaching Christchurch there was an announcement over the intercom.

"We wish to welcome you to this fast service to London Waterloo, stopping at Southampton Central, Southampton Parkway, Woking, Clapham Junction and London Waterloo, and inform you that the refreshment car is now open."

Bill got up and asked if I would like to take some liquid refreshment. I replied that I would love a cup of coffee and perhaps a little portion of fruitcake. Bill disappeared in the direction of the refreshment carriage, and I settled down to the soporific regularity of the sound of thundering metal wheel against metal track and gently nodded off to sleep. I was rudely awakened by an alarmed plea for assistance from Bill, who said that he had a very odd sensation of a warm dampness around his legs. Expecting the plainly obvious, that he had failed to visit the toilet on his way to get the coffee and cake, I asked him to sit down to see what the problem was. I didn't want him making a fuss in full view of the crowded carriage.

I quickly spotted the problem. He had placed the coffee containers on their sides in the British Rail paper carrier bags, causing a considerable leak of hot coffee onto his trouser legs and leaving a trail of coffee on the Network South West carpeting that disappeared into the distance and through to the next carriage. His response was one that will remain in my memory for years to come. He simply said, on retrieving his soggy disposable coffee cup that was contained in the coffee-drenched and rapidly disintegrating paper bag:

"I really think that the portions of British Rail coffee these days are a disgrace."

He drank the dregs from his cup whilst eating a very soggy fruitcake. I did the same while he produced two miniature bottles of brandy, which seemed to lighten the situation.

The rest of the journey was filled with conversational pleasantries. I briefly asked him what his dental problems were and he informed me that he was suffering terrible toothache from his molars. I pointed out to him that he had false teeth and therefore couldn't get toothache anymore.

He then informed me that all he had to do was to place his teeth in a glass and the pain in his mouth went away, and that the teeth ached in the glass by themselves. As the teeth were no longer attached to his gums, they only hurt in the glass and not in his mouth. When they were stuck to his gums they hurt. I had to accept this explanation, but began to realise that the purpose of this trip was to provide him with a new and better-fitting pair of teeth.

We duly arrived at the dental surgery and I made sure Bill was comfortably seated whilst I searched for the relief of a toilet. On my return I was staggered to find him stripped to the waist, with a very distinguished-looking lady searching through his shirt.

"Whatever is going on?" I asked.

I never knew what might happen whenever I left him alone in a crowded waiting room but this was going to require a pretty good explanation.

"This lady wished to know where I purchased this shirt as she would like to purchase a similar one for her husband," he replied. "As you know, I buy most of my clothes from the local charity shop and I had no idea of the origin of this particular shirt. This kind young lady explained that her husband had worn such a shirt about twenty-five years ago and she had always liked it and wanted to get another. She couldn't find the label on the collar so asked where the label was. When I told her it was probably around the bottom of the shirt she requested that I took it off rather than her having to search inside the top of my trousers."

I have to admit that the shirt was rather special, being of a sort of military appearance with loads of pockets and a very striking heavy stitching that gave the impression of added strength.

The lady added in a posh voice, "I really don't mind semi nudity, and I have been able to locate the maker of the garment.

"Please would you put your shirt back on, to save your friend's embarrassment; and thank you for being such a helpful, and I must say rather attractive, gentleman. I'm sorry, I didn't quite catch your name."

"William Treatham at your service, madam. I am pleased to have been able to assist. Here is my card. Please feel free to call me whenever you are in Poole."

I sat in stunned silence as Bill replaced his shirt. The rest of our time in Southampton was pretty uneventful, apart from a strange encounter in the local pub where we stopped for a bite to eat. Bill was his usual self, enjoying a pint of real ale, when a middle-aged lady came to sit by his side. She was heavily made-up and wore clothes that would have been more suited to a lady half her age. She deliberately hitched her skirt to above her knees as she sat down and looked longingly into Bill's eyes and said, in a broad Liverpool accent:

"I was just wondering whether you or your friend, or both of you, would care to 'turn a shilling'."

We both sat there totally bemused, wondering what she meant, until the landlord intervened and ordered the lady out of the pub. It turned out that her turn of phrase was an illusion to paying for some sexual favour and that she was a well-known local prostitute. I was a little shocked, but Bill was highly amused and castigated the landlord for throwing her out as he insisted he would have liked to have got to know her better and to have given her one of his cards. I quickly changed the subject and we ordered fish and chips for two.

The return journey was as eventful as the outward trip. Bill seemed to have the ability to engage complete strangers in conversation and soon had the whole carriage listening to his tales. Everything was fine, until a young lady on the seat in front of him decided to turn around, kneel on her seat and say:

"Would you like to see my belly button?"

Needless to say, I was shocked and horrified as he answered in the affirmative. She duly pulled up her top to reveal her navel and then asked again, completely unashamedly:

"And would you like one of my Jaffa cakes?"

As Bill took the Jaffa cake, the girl's mother turned and said to her, in a slightly amused tone:

"Samantha, how many times must I tell you not to speak to strange men? You really must realise that you are only three years old and people don't necessarily want to speak with you!" She obviously hadn't met Bill before.

Samantha spent the rest of the journey in conversation with Bill and readily dispensed most of her Jaffa cakes, which he ate with relish. The trip ended with him handing his card to Samantha's mum.

4th September 2008

Please please me

The role of team leader can be very interesting but equally embarrassing and potentially job destroying. I well remember some very embarrassing moments whilst carrying out my duties in performing risk assessments. One such ordeal was at the hands of Daphne Prendergast, who had asked for help every morning to assist in her morning ablutions. I had already found the availability of staff to enable the calls to take place at eight in the morning as requested, and needed to check out her flat and her abilities. This was necessary before the care package commenced so as not to put either her or our staff in any unnecessary danger.

I arrived at her address at the agreed time and entered into a lengthy description as to why I was there and what I hoped to achieve. I was there to assess safety issues within her home and also to find the level and capability of her mobility and her needs concerning any aids she might want. All was well so far. Daphne gave me the impression of a once lively and outgoing young lady, who had lived gracefully to the grand age of eighty-nine. She was completely 'with it' mentally and possessed a rather wicked sense of humour, as I was to discover later in the assessment.

I checked her electrical equipment for any defects and explained that she would need to have any portable appliances, such as kettles, irons and vacuum cleaners, PAT tested. She asked what Pat had to do with it and I explained that it stood for Portable Appliance Testing. I then checked carpets and rugs for any trip hazards, and lino and wooden floors for any slip hazards. I assessed the entrances and exits, and generally checked her flat for anything that might present a danger for either her or our staff. I noted that the bathroom floor might be slippery when wet – an oft-used phrase in personal details files.

It was necessary to assess her abilities as far as her mobility was concerned, and I asked her to do the usual procedures, such as standing from a seated position and sitting from a standing position. We then tried walking around the room, which proved difficult without some aids, so we tried it with a Zimmer frame and then with a rollator. No problems there, and all seemed okay.

The next exercise was to assess her ability to go from the lounge to the bedroom and thence to the bathroom, where we would need to do some serious assessment. We managed the former and made the bedroom, where she seemed a little unsure of herself and sat on the bed looking somewhat exhausted but with a very mischievous look in her eyes that was impossible to ignore. She was almost beckoning me to join her on the bed, perhaps to discuss in more detail what I was trying to achieve. Needless to say, my professionalism cut in and I suggested we proceed to the bathroom.

I wish I had instead decided to call an end to the visit and ask for a female carer to attend the risk assessment. Once in the bathroom I sat her on the perching stool at the basin and asked her to try to reach the taps, flannel, soap, toothpaste, toothbrush, towels, etc. This she achieved with ease. The next task was to assess her ability to use the battery operated bath seat, and I duly asked her to sit on it. This is where the assessment began to unravel! I seriously thought I was imagining things when I heard her say:

"Would you prefer it if I removed my clothes?"

I was stunned into silence until she repeated:

"Would you like me to do this in a state of nudity, to lend some reality to the scenario?"

"No! No! No!" I replied, wondering what was going to be suggested next. "I am simply trying to assess your ability to access the bath; I really didn't intend to actually give you a bath. That is a task for the morning carers."

Her reply stunned me, although I have to admit that she did have a wicked glint in her eyes, suggesting she was winding me up.

"Well, I think you are really mean. My dear husband left me over twenty-six years ago, when he sadly died, and since then I haven't had a man in my bathroom to whom I can show my feminine charms – until now. It would be so much more realistic if I was to remove my clothes and actually have you perform my bathing routine."

I knew then, by the look on her face, that she was pulling my leg; and anyway, I explained to her, I didn't have the necessary protective equipment with me. I also had to reply that it would be most unprofessional, as I began to wonder how it would look if I had fulfilled her wishes. I could have found myself, hands in sudsy water, washing a naked woman's back when my boss walked in to check up on me! It would probably have meant instant dismissal and maybe even a criminal record.

However, I managed to persuade her to show me how she managed the seat whilst fully clothed, and I duly put my submission in her notes, with the addition that a male carer should never be sent to this address. I also asked that female team leaders were in future used for her assessments, although I never explained why.

Which reminds me of an incident involving a car and an unexpected journey.

2nd March 2009

An unexpected journey

Everything was going as expected in our busy office. Whilst I preferred to be out in the field on beautiful sunny days like today, I always welcomed the chance to sit in quiet contemplation of tasks completed during hours of work. I had completed three risk assessments and four personal care plans for various clients across Dorset. It had required quite a lot of travel, and I was glad to be back towards the end of the day and ready to get back to the comfort of home.

As I was finishing writing my reports I was just a little annoyed to hear the service manager call me into her office.

"Please could you call at the Sunnyholme Care Home before you finish for the day? It is on your way home and will only take a few minutes."

"What is involved?" I asked, feeling a little apprehensive, as I knew the layout of this particular home and the difficulties in parking and also finding the correct room in the labyrinth of corridors.

"We have been asked to take the service user out on a weekly basis for shopping expeditions and a drive along the coast. It just requires a risk assessment of her ability to access the car, and the safety issues involved with taking her away from her environment."

It was very difficult to say no to our manager, as she didn't quite understand the meaning of the word. However, alarm bells began to ring in my head as I imagined the problems that could be associated with such a task and the risk that something might go wrong, ending with the inevitable call to the paramedics and the compiling of an accident form, should such an occurrence happen. As always, I shrugged my shoulders and said okay.

I still had half an hour of work time and hoped I could finish the task in time. Our organisation had no concept of the idea of overtime.

I managed to find a convenient parking space at the home straight away, so maybe this wasn't going to be as bad as expected. I made my way to the reception desk and enquired as to the whereabouts of Alice Thompson. They were expecting me and guided me to the furthest room situated on the furthest corridor from the car park.

Without seeming rude or offensive I have to say that I really wasn't expecting Alice to be of such a robust girth, and began to wonder whether she would get into the passenger seat of my not over large car. I was also a little apprehensive when she stated that she would make the long walk to the car park using her rollator rather than a wheelchair, especially when I had noticed a large electric powered one outside her door, which would have taken away the task of pushing her in a manual one.

Reluctantly I agreed, as she insisted that she really needed the exercise. By this time all of the staff who had been bustling around previously seemed to vanish into thin air. I wondered if they knew something I didn't. However, we started on the very slow, laborious walk to the car park and about fifteen minutes later arrived at the front passenger door of my car.

"Where are we going?" asked Alice

"Nowhere today," I replied, thankful that once this assessment was completed and Alice was safely left at the reception area, I could make my way home. "I am merely here to assess your ability to get in and out of a car. I understand that in the recent past you were always provided with disabled transport, but the occupational therapist says you can manage with an ordinary car. If everything is alright we will be coming over each week to take you out."

"Oh, that sounds wonderful. Where are they going to take me?"

"Trips to the shops and perhaps a drive along the coast," I replied.

With those few words I set about installing a special extra handle into the door latch and a turntable pad on the seat and, after much huffing and puffing, managed to get her onto the passenger seat and close the door. I knew I could carry a wheelchair in the luggage compartment and a rollator on the rear seat. Satisfied that I had completed a successful assessment, I opened the door and attempted to get hold of her legs so that I could turn her around to enable her to pull herself to the standing position. I could see she was getting agitated and could see tears welling in her eyes.

"Whatever is the matter?" I asked.

"I think it's really rotten to put me through all the tiring walk and the awkward access to the car and then not even give me the pleasure of a ride around the block. It is such a long time since I had a proper car ride," she said, beginning to weep into her blouse.

I felt a sudden pang of remorse and found myself subconsciously putting her legs back into the car and placing myself in the driving seat. I called the care home reception on my mobile to inform them that I was taking Alice for a short ride to assess her reaction to being in a car on a busy road. Rather a weak explanation, but as I started the engine I could sense a happier person beside me.

"Only round the block, though," I said cautiously, realising that I had started something I might not be able to control easily. As we rounded the block and I was about to turn into the home, she exclaimed:

"Please don't take me home yet. I used to go to the Haven Point as a child and watch the fishing boats sailing in and out of the harbour. Please let's go there briefly. You would make an old lady very happy, and it's only a mile away!"

Reluctantly I turned the car away from the care home entrance and headed the three miles to Haven Point, on the edge of the Sandbanks peninsula. How anyone could imagine that a destination was one-third of its actual distance is beyond me, and the extra mileage was going to eat into my home time. However, I felt that I had to let Alice recall her youth.

We duly arrived, and I parked among the spaces used to view the harbour entrance between the English Channel and Poole Harbour. This gave a fine view of both Studland and the comings and goings of various marine traffic, which had to pass through this narrow channel to go about their marine business. I actually enjoyed sitting in this wonderful location and often came to this point on my own to contemplate my life and my current situation. I was in the middle of a maritime daydream when Alice shattered my peace by declaring:

"Did you realise that my beloved sister lived in Swanage?"

"No," I replied, temporarily taken aback by her sudden statement and the assumption that I might know her sister and where she lived. This was particularly surprising, as I had only made Alice's acquaintance about forty-five minutes earlier.

"As we are so close to Swanage could we just pop over there to see where she lived? She unfortunately died three years ago but she was very special to me."

"Do you realise how far we would have to go?" I replied. "The home will be worried about you if we stay away too long."

"It's only over the channel on the ferry and then we're there," she pleaded.

Reluctantly I started the car again and joined the queue for the Sandbanks/Swanage ferry. Whilst in the queue I phoned the home and the office to inform them of where we were going and what time I would be back. I had to pay for the ferry fare out of my own pocket, as there was no sign of Alice reaching for her purse. I have to admit that the trip to Swanage was most pleasurable, until we arrived outside her late sister's house, when she calmly announced that her other sister lived in Weymouth and could we please go there as we were already on the way.

I really had to put a stop to this madness. The home would begin to wonder whether I had kidnapped Alice, and they would have thrown away her supper. Also, I was eating into my home time and my dinner would be ruined by the time I got home from Weymouth. My immediate worry was that I didn't know how many sisters Alice had.

I could end up in Bridport and then forward to Devon and even Cornwall. I very quickly said that Swanage was as far as I was prepared to go today and that I would try to arrange a trip to Weymouth at a later date, pointing out that she would have to pay travel expenses. With that made clear I returned to the ferry and we made our way back to the care home.

I really regret that I had to pay for two ferry crossings, a load of petrol and a severe loss of time away from home. However, I did have the feeling that I had made a very elderly lady a little happier.

When I finally arrived home about two hours later I was greeted by the dulcet tones of my dear wife Angela, with the well-worn cliché: "The dinner's in the dog."

However, she was joking, but was a little cross that I hadn't phoned her to say I would be late. The dinner wasn't in the dog, as she had called the office to ask where I was. She knew that I had a very soft spot for anyone elderly and disabled, especially the ladies, and knew that they, in turn, could twist me round their little fingers.

The dog greeted me with his usual waggy tail enthusiasm and looked at me with his ever-hungry eyes, seemingly longing for me to sit down to dinner so that at least a small proportion of the delicious food would inevitably end up in the dog following his constant begging.

14th November 2006
An unexpected delivery

Following on from my unexpected journey, I must point out that many calls from a care worker to a service user can end up being classified as 'unexpected'. I have come across many unexpected situations during my time as a care worker, but probably none more so than the uncontrollable situation that occurred on 14th November 2006.

Today I have been sent on an unusual assignment. Mr Frederick Smyth, a gentleman of advanced age, requires some help this morning and for the next few weeks. Frederick, or Freddy as he likes to be known, lives with his granddaughter Jackie and her husband of two years, Jake. Freddy moved in with them as his health started to deteriorate and was assured of first-class care from Jackie, who idolised her grandpa. Jake was very helpful too, but had to go to work to fund the family commitments. Those commitments were about to increase dramatically as Jackie had become pregnant and was now in her ninth month. Hence the need for help, as she couldn't do all that was necessary, due to her increasing size, and when the baby arrived she would need some extra help.

I introduced myself to Freddy and couldn't help but wonder at the obvious bond between Grandpa and Granddaughter. It always heartens me when I see the younger generation caring for their precious old folk, not out of duty, but out of pure love. He had an amazing character and, like so many elderly people that I came across, never complained about his ailments and always showed his happy side.

I took an immediate liking to this close family unit and listened intently as Jackie explained exactly what she expected for the care of Grandpa. Jake left for work and Jackie settled down to a well-earned rest as I started the routine of washing, shaving and dressing. Freddy always wore a tie, whatever the weather, and it was whilst I was trying to tie this that Jackie appeared in the doorway. It was a long time since I had had to tie someone else's tie – probably my son's when he started school. It had to be tied in what was effectively a mirror image.

In my struggle I merely noticed Jackie's presence and continued in my task. It was only when I heard a cry of pain that I took notice of her. In what can only be described as a tone of increasing panic she explained that she felt she was about to deliver the baby. I didn't worry too much as I knew the gap after the first contraction meant that there was a long gap between the first contraction and actual birth. However, Jackie explained to me that she had been having pains all night and hadn't said anything as she didn't want to wake up Jake, as he had to go to work in the morning. She did feel that she was very near to giving birth and I tried not to show signs of panic.

I do have some experience of childbirth, but the look on Jackie's face caused me some alarm. My experience was restricted to the birth of both of my children. I had been present at both births, the first of which was my beloved daughter, Sarah. I had been at my wife Angela's bedside during labour at the local maternity hospital. Knowing very little at the time of such processes, I became alarmed at every contraction and pressed the alarm for some assistance. After about the tenth call, the alarm was confiscated and I was sent out of the delivery room until a more appropriate time. However, thankfully I was there at the birth and was able to witness one of life's miracles, albeit thinking to myself how grateful I was that men didn't have to undergo such a process.

The second instance was the birth of my equally beloved son, Peter. I was now wise to the process and was quite happy when a nurse escorted me out of the labour ward, as they were about to perform something that I misheard as an enigma, but later turned out to be an enema, which I later learned was something that I really wouldn't want to witness. Having been awake for some hours, I promptly fell asleep and had to be woken up to witness the birth of Peter, having missed all the painful contraction business. Again, a wonder of nature, and relief that I didn't have to go through the pain and distress of hard labour. However, I will never forget the look on Angela's face, which portrayed utter pride and love, and showed no sign of the pain of birth.

The only other birth experience I'd had was seeing a programme in the television series, *Dr. Finlay's Casebook*, which aired in the late 1950s on the BBC. In one episode the doctor was called to a premature birth concerning one of his patients. The midwife was unavailable and Dr Finlay was to perform the delivery, his first, under the instructions of a Dr Cruickshank, who was linked to the birth event by a very antiquated telephone system to his surgery at Arden House. I can remember the words issuing forth as if it were yesterday:

"Get plenty of fresh towels and as much hot water as possible. Don't forget to sterilise the scalpel for cutting the umbilical!"

Those words rang in my mind as I dialled 999 to get some urgent help with the situation, while Grandpa looked on without noticing my increasing panic, as the contractions seemed to get closer together.

I guided Jackie to the bedroom and noticed what must have been a breaking of the waters. This was turning serious! I then gathered as many towels as possible and filled many pots, pans and buckets with hot water. Realising that I wouldn't find a scalpel, I found a sharp pair of kitchen scissors, which I promptly immersed in boiling water for sterilisation.

As I re-entered the bedroom, imagine my shock and horror when I could see the clear outline of a baby's head emerging from Jackie's birth canal. Her cries of pain increased as I became aware that a birth was about to take place. As a care worker I had been trained in almost every problem that might occur, but never the delivery of a baby. All I could do was get the scissors at the ready and take hold of the many towels I had collected.

I have never been so relieved to hear an approaching siren as I was at this time. The paramedics arrived to find me assisting with the birth of a beautiful girl, and thankfully their professionalism took over and baby Louise was born to an unsuspecting world.

The first person to be presented with a very beautiful Louise, after her mum, was Grandpa, who was ecstatic, as this was his first great-grandchild. Then it was my turn and I felt, for no real reason, great pride that I had somehow assisted in this precious new life. The family remembered what I had done by inviting me to the christening ceremony some weeks later. I continued to care for Grandpa for the next few weeks, until Jackie felt able to continue her loving care of a very special grandpa.

7th June 2009
An unexpected death

To complete a trilogy of unexpected situations, it is necessary for me to mention a sudden death that occurred shortly before I visited Victor, husband of Gloria, to do a new risk assessment prior to her discharge from hospital following a knee replacement operation.

Whenever a service user returns from hospital it is necessary to conduct a new service plan and risk assessment to ensure that no new procedures or mobility equipment will be required.

Victor, a sprightly octogenarian, has been looking after the home whilst Gloria has been in hospital. One of his daily tasks has been to feed their beloved budgerigar, Joey, and let him out of his cage to fly around for his daily exercise. Joey, a very friendly bird, enjoys his time out in the lounge and sometimes ventures into the kitchen to investigate what may be around.

Before I became a team leader I used to call on Victor while he recovered from a very nasty illness. Joey always fascinated me, as he seemed to relish the company of humans and would often land on my head or shoulders whilst I was administering care. He would peck lightly at my ear and talk in budgie talk and sometimes managed a human word. Mostly, though, he was more interested in anything small enough to pick up in his beak, which he then tossed aside, unless it happened to be food.

Today a very concerned-looking Victor, who asks me straight away to go and look at Joey, as he seems to be motionless on the floor of his cage, meets me. I make my way into the lounge and find Joey, obviously deceased, with his little legs in the air.

"Whatever is the matter?" exclaimed Victor.

"I'm afraid he seems to be dead. He must have been quite old so I suppose it was inevitable at some time," I replied, trying to sound compassionate, as I knew they loved their precious bird.

"He can't be dead. Gloria will be devastated," he said, with an obvious lump in his throat. "You'll have to take him to the pet shop for me and try to find an exact match in colour and markings. If we can do that, Gloria will never be any the wiser."

Feeling that I would appear to be in some Monty Python sketch about dead parrots, I suggested that, rather than take poor Joey to the pet shop, I would take a photo of him and take that instead. What a blessing modern mobile phones can be when you find yourself in the position where you need an urgent photograph.

On arrival at the pet shop I explained the problem and showed them the photo. They took me through to a caged area, where I was pleased to see many green budgies, the same colour as Joey. We eventually found one that looked the image of a younger Joey, and I bought him and took him in a box to Victor, who had cleaned out the cage and carefully buried Joey at the top of the garden. The new bird, which was obviously also called Joey, seemed to settle well and looked the spitting image of poor old Joey, though a little younger. We were pleased with our morning's work and I promised to visit the next day to ensure that Gloria was settled.

The next morning I duly arrived to find Victor talking to the bird, imploring him not to give the game away. After about twenty minutes the ambulance arrived with Gloria; she gave Victor a massive kiss on the cheek and then proceeded straight to the lounge to be reunited with her beloved bird. As she got to the cage she recoiled in horror.

"That's not Joey! Where is my precious Joey?"

It took a lot of explaining, but I think in the end she bowed to the inevitable, and I left, reasonably happy that I had managed to get Victor out of a very sticky situation.

A week later I re-visited to make sure that everything was okay, and found Gloria in deep conversation with her new bird.

6th April 2009

Storm clouds on the horizon

All is not well within our beloved country, as the economy seems to be slipping into a dangerous phase and is experiencing a severe downturn. Banks have had to be rescued by the government and the world seems to be facing a dreaded recession, which has not been known for many years. It is inevitable that we are about to enter a period of austerity, the like of which we have not seen since the war years.

I feel deeply concerned for the care sector. We have an increasingly ageing population, bringing increasing demand for care services. Also, advances made in medical science mean that people are living longer and are being cured of illnesses that previously led to the end of life.

As the Chair of Poole Council's Health and Social Care Overview and Scrutiny Committee, I am already seeing signs of weakness in our ability to cope with the ever-increasing demand. Those people with moderate care needs are no longer receiving funding, having to care for themselves or rely on relatives and friends. This often leads to a rapid deterioration in their condition, which means they are no longer classed as moderate and move swiftly into a higher categories, meaning they then qualify for funding.

Government funding is not increasing and is failing to take account of inflation. This means that covering the extra needs is impacting on local authorities, which are no longer able to increase funding to care organisations. Wages of care staff are static, and recruitment and retention of care staff is getting evermore difficult. This is leading to some organisations becoming unviable.

I am convinced that we are heading for a severe crisis in the care sector, and say, at every opportunity, that a civilized country should always consider the care of its elderly, disabled and vulnerable people an absolute funding priority.

Unfortunately, it appears that the reverse is the case and that the sector seems to be an easy area to make savings. I have warned on many occasions that if care staff are not paid a proper living wage, being able to exist without wondering how they are going to meet their expenses, they will be forced to leave, with dire consequences for those who really need us.

During most of my time with my employers I have been a staff representative on the National Staff Association of our care organisation. I was appointed, some years ago, onto the National Executive Committee, representing care at home staff across the United Kingdom. The association represents some 7,000 staff nationally, and my new position enabled me to see at first-hand how the organisation was doing.

At a recent meeting we received a report from our fairly newly appointed chief executive. He had literally been brought in to save the well-known charity from the difficulties that lay ahead; a mammoth task considering they have over 200 services dotted around the UK. What he had to say was not pleasing and would have repercussions on me personally. I have worked my way up through my service to become a team leader. The boss now says that we are going to have to cope with fewer administrative staff, fewer leaders and more care assistants. The writing is clearly on the wall for some of the staff in our local care at home service.

I returned to work the next day with a heavy heart. I knew that we could be expecting some job losses and that at least one team leader faced redundancy. I felt that I must bite the bullet and accept redundancy, as the other team leaders had family commitments that I no longer experienced. I would be the one to have to go, along with at least two posts in administration.

Sure enough, it was announced the next day that in our service there were to be cuts in staff and that at least one team leader faced the axe. That would be me; and although I faced my fate with optimism for the future, I couldn't help feeling acutely sad that I was leaving so many past and present clients.

They had taught me so much over the years. They had taught me tolerance, patience, understanding, humility and pride; humility because of their stoicism, and pride that I was able to connect with them, no matter what the disability.

I had laughed with them, even cried with them, experienced their lows and their highs, their happy times and their sad times. I had experienced that key message: that disabled people were not different but had a wealth of experience to impart to everyone. I had been through happy times and incredibly sad times, when I had joined them in celebration and happiness, or grieved with them or their families.

I would miss all this and more, but would continue to visit those whom I had grown close to, for as long as they still wanted to see me. Happily for me, I was about to enter a new phase in my life that was to consume my entire being for the next two years.

I had recently been elected to the position of Sheriff of Poole and was to be installed at the beginning of May. I had also been voted Chair of the Dorset Fire Authority, but most importantly I remained as Chair of the Health and Social Care Committee, which enabled me to keep in touch with the on-going problems within the sector. I was also involved with the

South West Healthcare Trust, as it was then, so I was able to get a wider picture.

The post of Sheriff of Poole was first established under the Great Charter of Elizabeth I in 1568, which gave extensive powers and privileges to the town. This was the charter that gave Poole the status of 'County and Town', which meant it was separate from the County of Dorset. It was therefore the Elizabethan equivalent of a unitary authority.

Only nineteen towns were ever granted this status, although many cities enjoyed the privilege. Apart from the various powers granted to the County and Town of Poole, specific provision was made for the appointment of the post of sheriff, elected annually, each November. The sheriff serves a year in the post, following which the post-holder is elevated to the position of mayor.

With the decline of the powers of the monarch, and centralising powers being introduced by parliament, it necessarily affected the powers and role of the sheriff.

The post became a ceremonial one following the passing of the Local Government Act 1972, which was implemented on 1st April 1974 when Poole became a district council. Queen Elizabeth II granted a new charter, allowing the post of sheriff to continue. However, in the mid-90s Poole became a unitary authority and regained the status that allowed it to run its own affairs, such as social care services, education, transportation, and many others. This meant that it had regained the status to be called a county in its own right.

The sheriff, upon election (now in May), is formally presented with the symbols of his former powers: the staff (or wand), surmounted with a crown signifying the former connection to the Crown; a key, symbolically representing the past duty of the keeper of the town gaol; and the chain of office, which dates from the 1880s and contains thirty-seven links.

Although the powers of the sheriff have long since gone, it is appropriate that Poole still preserves the tradition of the post, which prepares the post-holder for the honour of becoming the mayor, for the benefit of the town.

Once installed as sheriff, I often accompanied the mayor on various engagements, including citizenship ceremonies and a visit to a Buckingham Palace garden party.

I often regretted that the sheriff no longer had the power to send miscreants to jail or put vandals or troublemakers in the stocks or pillory.

The human treadmill was long gone, as were the town gallows. Thankfully, all justice was now in the safe hands of the constabulary and the Courts of Justice. Whilst it would have been great to administer my own justice to some of the people I came across, it would be very dangerous to put that sort of power into the hands of one man.

As Chair of the Dorset Fire Authority, I made it my goal to visit every fire station and station watch in the county and to personally meet as many of the fire fighters as possible. Whilst the running of the fire and rescue service was in the capable hands of the chief fire officer, the authority decided policy and financial issues, and great strides were made during my chairmanship, where we became one of the best run authorities in the country while being among the worst funded. This was in no small measure due to the professionalism of the chief fire officer and his deputies, as well as a superb staff of frontline men and women and a strong administrative workforce. It was an absolute honour to work with them all and to temporarily become a member of the Fire Brigade family.

As the chair, I also became a peer assessor for the Improvement and Development Agency, advising other chairs of any actions needed to improve their services and ready themselves for Audit Commission inspections. I also sat on the

Fire Forum of the Local Government Association and became a member of the National Olympic Security Committee, which looked into security for the forthcoming Olympic Games to be held in London. The reason for my appointment to this committee was because the sailing events were to be held at Weymouth in the County of Dorset.

I was proud of the authority's achievements during my tenure. We saw three new fire stations, a new headquarters, new divisional office for the main conurbation in the county, and safer fire fighting outfits for our frontline staff, as well as new improved breathing apparatus. More importantly, we saw a decline in the number of fires, together with fewer injuries and fatalities. It became a reachable target to have smoke alarms in every household in Dorset, with the fire service offering free supply and fitting of the alarms.

I had truly entered a gilded bubble on leaving the care sector, and duly became Mayor of Poole in 2010, carrying out around 600 engagements over my mayoral year. But that is another book in the making for the future.

I end by expressing my admiration for the many care workers across the UK, whether working in service users' homes or in care homes.

We also shouldn't forget the many people who care for their own relatives and friends. They do this out of love and devotion and receive no reward, apart from knowing that they are making a better life for those in need.

There is also a large number of forgotten carers who go to great lengths under enormous difficulties to look after their sick or disabled loved ones. I talk of the band of young carers who often rush home from school to tend to their family members in need of help.

It would be remiss of me not to mention a young carers' champion that I had the pleasure to know over many years.

Ray Smith, a local councillor and past Mayor of Poole, went out of his way to celebrate young carers and to highlight their valuable contribution to society.

Whilst I was Mayor of Poole I got to witness his dedication first-hand. I accompanied him and dozens of helpers and children on a boat trip and lunch to Swanage. I also attended his young carers' children's disco, where each child received a present. I spoke to many of the young carers and they told me that Ray made them feel special and wanted.

To this day I don't know how he funded these special events, but have a suspicion that he wasn't afraid to use his own money. I was so glad that he received an award from the Queen. Never has such a reward been so richly deserved.

All carers do so much to make our country a better place, and rarely seek praise or reward for what they do. Those who work in the care sector do so, not to enrich themselves, but to enrich the lives of those they help. Thank you, one and all.